Care of Bees in Warré and Top Bar Hives

by
Joe Bleasdale

Care of Bees in Warré and Top Bar Hives
© 2014 Joe Bleasdale

All rights reserved. No part of this publication may be reproduced, stored in a retrieval system, transmitted in any form or by any means electronic, mechanical, including photocopying, recording or otherwise without prior consent of the copyright holders.

ISBN 978-1-908904-58-4

Published by Northern Bee Books, 2014
Scout Bottom Farm
Mytholmroyd
Hebden Bridge
HX7 5JS (UK)

Design and artwork
D&P Design and Print
Worcestershire

Printed by Lightning Source, UK

Care of Bees in Warré and Top Bar Hives

by
Joe Bleasdale

Northern Bee Books

Care of Bees in Warré and Top Bar Hives

A guide for new beekeepers and for beekeepers who have acquired the increasingly popular Warré and Top Bar Hives and those who want to stop using chemicals. This book is also for anyone who would like to know more about these marvellous creatures and the art of beekeeping. Many new beekeepers lose their bees because they do not understand them. They may read books on the mystery and magic of bees, but not how to care for a hive of bees. This book gives practical guidance with clear instructions, line drawings, and photographs.

- Essential knowledge of the lifecycle of the honeybee
- Details of essential equipment
- Beekeeping activities throughout the year
- Disease, swarming and honey production

It has advice from my 30 years beekeeping not found in standard books on beekeeping:

- colony stress in spring
- swarm collection
- winter survival
- varroa control without chemicals
- propagation of varroa-resistant colonies
- HONEY without STRESS

I do not use chemicals for varroa or other diseases. They poison the bees and make them weak. Would you like honey from hives that have residues of chemicals: oxalic acid, formic acid, flumethrin, thymol, fluvalinate etc? That is like chemical warfare, not ecology! For research on the harm to the viability of queens and drone semen see reference 2 below. In 2000 I stopped using chemicals, and my losses through varroa have decreased. Many beekeepers still lose colonies through winter deaths, failing queens, paralysis etc. I believe many of these losses are caused by chemicals that weaken the bees.

Since varroa came to Britain in 1992, beekeepers have used a variety of medicines. Some have been partially effective, but since they do not exterminate all varroa, varroa have evolved to become resistant to them. Similar to superbugs in hospitals that are resistant to antibiotics, beekeepers have bred RESISTANT VARROA. They should be breeding RESISTANT BEES.

1. Signs of Varroa Resistance:
   http://www.youtube.com/watch?v=xk7duoVoaKg
2. Lisa Marie Burley: The Effects of Miticides on the Reproductive Physiology of Honey Bee (*Apis mellifera L.*) Queens and Drones
   http://scholar.lib.vt.edu/theses/available/etd-08162007-092313/unrestricted/lmburley.pdf

v13 © 2014
Joe Bleasdale

Hive Overflow!
Photo by Sarah Ellis August 2010

Acknowledgements

I would like to thank the following, who have given permission for the use of their colour photographs:

1. Paul Brennan of Limerick Beekeepers in Eire, an organisation that is committed to advance the use of the native Irish Black Bee.
   Web site: http:/limerickbees.net/
2. Dr. Mary Coffey, Teagasc, Oakpark Research Centre, Carlow

Title page photographs taken by the author

Contents

Introduction 1
    Benefits and Joys of Beekeeping 3
    No Fuss? 3
    Why no chemicals? 4
    Who should keep bees? 7
    Urban Beekeeping 7
    Stings 7

The Lifecycle of the Honey Bee 9
    Beehive in Nature 9
    Sexes 10
    The Queen 11
        Swarming 11
        Supersedure 13
        Emergency Queen Cells 14
        What to do about Swarming? 14
    Drones 15
    Workers 16
    Pollen and Nectar 18
    Senses and Communication 19
        Sight 19
        Smell and Taste 19
        Hearing and Touch 20
        Magnetism 20
    Races of Honey Bees 20

A Year in the Hive 23
    Winter 23
    Spring 23
    Summer 24
    Autumn or Fall 25

The Artificial Hive 26
    Skep Hives 27
    Modern Hives 27
        The Nucleus 27
        Top Bar Hives 27

The Warré Hive 27
The Horizontal Top Bar Hive 29
Caution 30
Pros and Cons of Warré and HTB 31

Starting Beekeeping 34
Safety Precautions 34
Essential Equipment 35
Collecting the Hive 35
Setting up a Top Bar Hive: Hiving a Swarm 37

Seasonal Activities 42
Check Stores 43
Inspection 45
The Swarm Dilemma 45
Failure to raise a queen 47
Taking Some Honey 47
Extracting the Honey 50
Comb honey 51
Honey crystallised in the comb 54
Composition of honey 54
Wax Extraction 57
Preparing for Winter 57
Ventilation 58

Unplanned Activities 59
Emergency Feeding 59
Spring Feeding 59
Autumn Feeding 60
Colonies under Stress - Nosema 61
Inspection of Brood 63
Swarm Warning 65
Laying Workers 67
Relocating a Hive 69

Brood Diseases 70
American foulbrood 70
European foulbrood 70
Other common brood diseases 70

Varroa **72**
   Treatment for Varroa 72
   Signs of Resistance to Varroa 72

Other Hive Pests **76**
   Wasps 76
   Mice 76
   Woodpeckers 76
   Large Mammals 76
   Wax Moth 76

Other Seasonal Operations **78**
   Combining Hives 78
   Winter Starvation 79
   Post Mortem 81
   Propagation 81
   Propagation of Varroa Resistance within a
   Local Beekeeping Association 82

Collecting a Swarm **83**
   The Ideal Swarm 83
   Hiving the Swarm 85
   Transferring Comb to a Frame 88
   Colonies in Buildings and Trees 90

Bee Friendly Environment **92**
The Joys of Beekeeping **94**
Further Reading **95**

ANNEX **97**
1. Colony Losses since stopping Chemical Treatment ... **97**
2. Winter Death Post Mortems **99**
3. Herbal Remedy for Nosema **100**

Tales of Swarms **102**
- a few anecdotes from my early days in beekeeping, with lessons learnt!

INDEX **111**

Introduction

This book is for those who would like to keep bees, but think that they may lack the time and resources. Beekeeping is indeed an absorbing activity and time spent observing these marvellous and productive insects can be instructive and fulfilling. But bees can fend for themselves and only need attention at critical times of the season. Too much interference is bad for them.

Many people have become interested in beekeeping recently, having heard and read about the plight of bees in the news and on television programmes. Beekeeping has become a fashionable hobby, but a large proportion of enthusiastic beginners have been discouraged, following losses of their colonies from various causes: disease, swarming, starvation, attacks by wasps, and that modern affliction, the varroa mite. Other reasons for people giving up have been poor seasons with no honey, lack of confidence in their ability to care for a hive, and so on.

I have tried to keep the book simple, describing in detail the essential operations. A hive of bees is a single organism and unnecessary operations harm its integrity. I have omitted some traditional practices said to prevent swarming, such as opening the hive every ten days or so in summer, to examine the brood frames and destroy queen cells. In my view this is futile: akin to cutting off dandelion heads hoping to prevent them flowering and setting seed. Bees intent on swarming will swarm anyway, and all the beekeeper achieves is unnecessary disturbance of the bees, an angry hive and a reduction of the honey crop. After all, swarming is the natural way that bees reproduce and evolve. Why suppress this instinct?

Much can be learned about the state of a hive by close observation of the bees flying in and out of the entrance. Pollen on the legs of bees will indicate brood present and a laying queen. Debris on the ground below and in front of the hive will tell a lot about their state of hygiene: removal of old comb, pollen, pupae, damaged varroa mites, etc. Dead or crawling bees unable to fly may indicate disease or the presence of varroa. One can check whether the hive is crowded and needs another box (Warré) or top bar (HTB), or whether it is about to swarm, just by quietly lifting the roof and looking over the top of the crown board, without delving into the brood box and letting cold air chill the brood.

In this book I will show you how to keep bees with a minimum of fuss and expense, to enjoy an absorbing and productive hobby. Another important aim, often forgotten by the hobbyist beekeeper, is to get a good crop of honey! The practices I describe are based on over thirty years experience with my bees in the counties of Hampshire and Somerset in England. There is no prescriptive rule for beekeeping that will guarantee success, but there are some principles that will guide the beekeeper on what actions to take in given circumstances. These I have described in this book.

Benefits and Joys of Beekeeping

Beekeeping is an enjoyable and absorbing hobby. There is always something new to learn and observe in these fascinating and useful insects. You will benefit from the products of the hive: delicious and healthy honey, beeswax that can be used for all manner of things, and other products that are used in cosmetics and medicines. You will meet fellow beekeepers and make new friends who have a like-minded regard and love of nature. Your bees will benefit the local environment by pollinating fruit, seeds and berries to produce food for people and wild life. You will develop a better understanding of nature and help make the world a better place.

There are few moments in life that match the joy and satisfaction of standing near a healthy hive on a warm day, when the bees are flying and bringing in their loads of sweet nectar and colourful pollen. To hear the humming of the hive and smell the intoxicating aroma of the evaporating nectar on a warm summer evening gives a feeling of peace and tranquillity that is rarely experienced in our mundane and hectic modern world: a true communion with nature.

No Fuss?

I believe that beekeeping should follow a happy mean between unnecessary intervention and neglect. For example, in my early days of beekeeping we were advised to open up the hive and inspect it every 10 days during the swarming season, to examine the brood chamber for queen cells which indicate that the hive is due to swarm, and take appropriate action. Frequent inspection of the brood chamber does cause stress to the colony, as will be explained in later chapters. The observant beekeeper can determine the state of the hive without having to disturb the bees, just by quietly lifting the roof and looking above the crown board: whether the hive is becoming crowded, for example, and needs another chamber for brood or honey. Observing the bees in front of the hive entrance will tell a lot about their health: whether they are infested with varroa, or infected with disease such as nosema or paralysis.

While I advise against unnecessary intervention, I do not advocate neglect. Uncontrolled swarming can be a nuisance to your neighbours, as well as loss of honey and possible loss of the colony. Each hive must be checked for brood disease during the season, definitely if requested by the appointed district bee inspector. Notification of foulbrood is a legal requirement in most counties, including the UK. Should your neighbours report a swarm, as a beekeeper you should be prepared to collect it if possible, whether or not it came from your hive. This book aims to give the optimum approach to productive and enjoyable beekeeping, based on the understanding of the nature of the honeybee and the colony as a sentient organism within our environment.

Why no chemicals?

In 2005, five years after I stopped treating my hives with chemicals, I wrote to the British Beekeepers Association Newsletter, proposing that all British beekeepers stop chemical treatment so that our native bees could evolve to resist varroa. The letter was published and responded to by Richard Ball, Acting National Bee Inspector. Though the need to treat varroa in the same way as the European beekeepers was necessary when it first arrived from the continent, it soon became apparent that the initial treatment, Bayvarol™, was becoming less effective as varroa developed a resistance to the chemical. So new chemicals were tried, with varying degrees of success: Apistan™, Apiguard™, oxalic acid, formic acid, and other thymol based medications. Varroa then developed a resistance to these chemicals, and the chemicals also weakened the bees, as would be expected. The 'cure' was worse than the disease, and it didn't eliminate varroa.

At the time I wrote my first letter, there was evidence of 'wild' colonies in buildings and hollows that managed to survive from year to year without any human intervention. In fact my own empty hives became occupied by their swarms, and were managing to thrive and produce honey without any medication. Some did succumb to varroa, but an increasing proportion managed to survive. My proposed solution, to cease chemical treatment, was ignored by all but a few far-sighted beekeepers, including Ron Hoskins who pioneered the Swindon Bee Project for propagating Varroa Resistant bees. Around that time arose the Natural Beekeeping movement, with its principles of non- intervention in the lifecycle of the hive. But the majority of British beekeepers continued to follow the practices advocated by the BBKA and poison their hives with varroicides. Their colony losses continued to rise and honey yields decline. Four years after that first correspondence I sent another letter giving details of my experience and my methods for over-wintering hives.

Below is the correspondence from the BBKA News of 2005 and 2009.

BBKA News
FREE TO MEMBERS OF THE BRITISH BEEKEEPERS' ASSOCIATION No. 154
AUGUST 2005

A Radical Solution
We seem to be spending a great deal of time and effort in trying to mitigate the problems of varroa. Now that varroa has become resistant to the chemical treatment, we are trying other methods, all of which cause distress to the bees.

I propose a radical solution: Leave them alone! Yes, colonies will die, but if they cannot resist the varroa by their own strategies, such as swarming or actively removing the mite themselves, then they are not fit, so good riddance. After a few years only resistant colonies will thrive. If varroa can build up resistance, so can our bees!
Joe Bleasdale, Somerset BKA

In Response
I would agree with Joe Bleasdale that leaving *Apis mellifera* and Varroa destructor 'to it' has the merit that only stocks and mites able to maintain a symbiotic relationship would survive.

This equilibrium exists with varroa's natural host Apis cerana. However, it is important to consider other possible implications to our environment. A full debate would fill a book but a précis would centre on the value bees represent to pollination. It is often claimed that every third mouthful of our food is reliant on insect pollination some, of course, being by Bombus and other bee species, which are not adversely effected by varroa. However, Defra have put a farm gate value, in England, of pollination by honey bees at £120,000,000 which may be conservative as many experts suggest a higher monetary value. Carreck and Williams estimated £200,000,000 for the United Kingdom.

Following the discovery of varroa in the UK beekeepers used pyrethroid treatments where they realised that varroa infestations were present and losses did not exceed 50%. If varroa were to be left uncontrolled we do not know the survival rate but it would be negligible, probably less than 1%. As a result many honey bee pollinated crops would fail resulting in a food production crisis and perhaps affecting the well being of man. Can we accept such a risk? This has been illustrated this season in California, USA, where high losses of honey bees have meant that it has been necessary to tranship bees from Florida and import bees from Australia to make up the difference to ensure pollination of almond crops. Then there is the economic threat to the beekeeping industry and people's livelihoods to consider.

Primarily man has caused varroa infestations in our bee colonies by interference with species boundaries. We must accept responsibility and control varroa levels ensuring that bees do not suffer any ill effects and can maintain their place within our ecostructure. As beekeepers it is our duty to monitor our bees and select strains that show tolerance to varroa. In this way we can accelerate a timetable to develop the same symbiotic relationship that Joe Bleasdale suggests in a rapid, dramatic and perhaps damaging way.
Richard Ball, Acting National Bee Inspector

BBKA - Supporting Bees and Beekeepers
FREE TO MEMBERS OF THE BRITISH BEEKEEPERS' ASSOCIATION NO.178 AUGUST 2009

What is Best for the Bees?
You kindly published my letter in the BBKA News of August 2005, with a response by Richard Ball, who explained why it was necessary to continue treating our bees for varroa. During the previous and intervening years I have tried a wide range of approved treatments and I am still of the opinion that we are doing more harm than good, both to our bees and to the environment. Invariably the hives that I have treated have either succumbed over winter, or went into a severe decline. Those that I left alone have fared well.

My present colonies are all from swarms that have entered my empty hives during the past three years, saving me the bother of collecting them. They are docile and productive and probably came from a feral colony in a nearby wood, though I have not yet located it. I over winter each hive by placing an empty super on the bottom, above which I place a queen excluder. This keeps the mice out, for I have found mice guards to be ineffective. It also prevents dropped varroa from circulating in the brood chamber. I have found it unnecessary to feed my bees, for there is a strong late autumn honey flow. The best help that the Government can give to beekeepers is to encourage a more sustainable environment, through planting orchards, hedges, woodlands with lime and sweet chestnut and nectar bearing crops like clover, lucerne and sunflower. Then our bees can look after themselves in a land of plenty.
Joe Bleasdale, Somerset BKA

Who should keep bees?

To keep bees you should be reasonably fit and healthy. You should be even-tempered, calm and gentle when checking the hive, and not the type of person to be flustered or panic when a cloud of bees is flying around you. Nor should you be careless or foolhardy, for it is bad for you and the bees if you are badly stung because you fail to make your bee suit bee-proof, or you open the hive in unsuitable weather and without using the smoker. You should be observant, noting the behaviour of the bees at the hive entrance, what they are bringing in to the hive or taking out from it. Though the philosophy of beekeepers with Top Bar Hives is minimum intervention, it is not an excuse for neglect.

Urban Beekeeping

There is a growing body of urban and city beekeepers who keep hives in secluded plots in gardens, allotments and even sheltered roof tops, and many report good crops of honey. The average temperature in cities is higher than in the countryside. There is also a wide variety of nectar and pollen bearing plants and trees in parks, gardens and derelict waste ground. Unlike agricultural land they are free of insecticides and herbicides. See my remarks about the environment in the Annex.

Stings

Though every precaution should be taken to prevent stings, a few stings during the season are almost inevitable. They will hurt to begin with, but most people will find that they become less painful as the season progresses. Despite all precautions, if the bees become angry when the hive is open, then close it up quickly and calmly and leave the hive alone for the day. A few stings to the hands can be tolerated, but a sting to the head, particularly near the eyes or mouth, can be serious. Therefore it is essential to have bee-proof headgear, and wear it at all times when at the hive.

If the sting is still attached to your skin, remove it immediately by scraping it off with a fingernail, because it will continue to inject venom and attract other bees to the spot through the odour it emits. Stings may be treated with a squirt of proprietary spray such as Wasp-eze™ aerosol, and if very painful take an anti-histamine pill and put an ice cube on the affected area. Rarely, some people may go into anaphylactic shock. Some beekeepers become sensitised after frequently being stung, and as a result may become prone to anaphylactic shock. That is a good reason for not disturbing the bees unnecessarily. Keep manipulations to the minimum and wear clean bee-tight clothing. The symptoms and advice for treating anaphylactic shock can be found on a suitable web site such as the British Beekeepers Association, link: http://www.bbka.org.uk/help/stings/anaphylactic_shock

The Lifecycle of the Honey Bee

Beehive in Nature

Honeybees are social insects and live in colonies of up to 80,000 bees. A colony will occupy hollow spaces in tree trunks, empty chimneys, and cavities in rocks or walls or roofs. Their main requirement is protection from the weather and a narrow entrance that can be defended against predators large and small: insects, birds and mammals. There should be enough space to accommodate the bees and their stores – at least a cubic foot (30 litres). Such suitable places will be sought by a swarm, which originates from an established hive. The swarm consists of between ten thousand to forty thousand bees. They will have ingested honey into their stomachs, some of which they will later convert into wax through glands in their abdominal segments. They form a hanging cluster after leaving the hive, or they may fly directly to their new home and cluster again, hanging from the top of the cavity. Within the warmth at the centre of the cluster they will produce wax and cooperate in moulding the wax into comb – see figure below.

They will start with a single comb and build parallel combs in a vertical plane running either side at about 1.44 inch (3.7 cm) separation. Each comb is made with a central sheet with interlocking hexagonal cells on each side of the sheet. The cells are used as stores for the bees food: honey and pollen, and also the bee brood: eggs, larvae and pupa. When raising brood, the bees must maintain the temperature inside the cluster where the brood is developing at 35 degrees centigrade: nearly the same as our own body temperature. This is an important point to bear in mind when the beekeeper is inspecting the hive, and a good reason for only opening the hive when necessary, and then only in warm weather. Don't fuss with the bees!

In addition to making wax, bees use propolis, an aromatic sticky resin collected from various plant materials. It has antiseptic and anti-fungal properties and it is applied within the hive to close up any cracks in the woodwork and to reduce drafts and the ingress o f moisture and predators such as wasps and other bees.

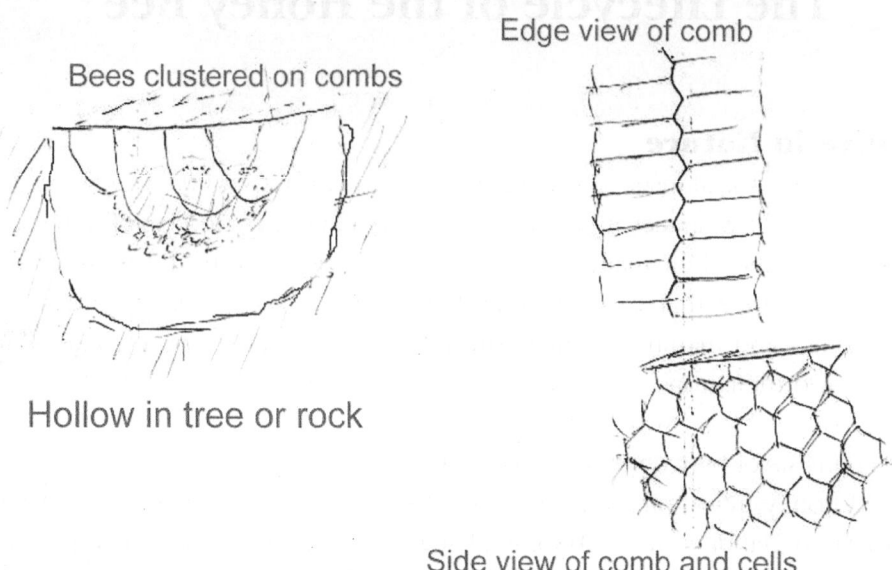

Bees and comb in natural hive

Sexes

There are three classes of honeybee in a hive: queen, drone and worker. The queen and the worker are female and they come from a fertilised egg, the drone is male and it comes from an unfertilised egg. The fertilisation is done just before the egg is laid, by a single sperm cell from a sac called a *spermatheca*. It is in the queen's abdomen and it holds all the semen that the queen received from the drones that mated with her on her mating flights. The drone comes from an unfertilised egg that is normally laid in the outer cells of the comb, which are larger than the inner cells (worker cells). The determination of the sexes was first discovered by Johann Dzierzon, a Catholic priest, in 1845. See the chapter "Further Reading", reference 7. It is remarkable how many beekeeping pioneers were clergymen!

The interval between the laying of the egg and the emergence of the bee from the pupal state is fixed for each class of bee. That is why the colony tries its utmost to maintain the temperature around the brood near a constant 35 degree C, whatever the outside weather conditions, and why it is harmful to open the hive in cold or windy weather. Hence you should only open the hive to look in the brood chamber for a necessary purpose. These are the development times in the lifecycle from the laying of the egg to the emergence of the young insect from the pupa:

Queen: 16 days
Drone   24 days
Worker   21 days

The Queen

In a well-regulated hive, the queen is the only one who lays eggs, one to a cell. The queen can live for up to six years, or until she runs out of eggs or semen (sperm). About 10 days after hatching she will make up to a dozen or so mating flights, far from the hive to mate with drones from other hives. They will provide her with enough semen for the rest of her life, to fertilise nearly a million eggs during the coming seasons, and she will never mate again. During the spring and summer, a vigorous queen could lay up to a thousand eggs a day. She will reduce her rate of laying in autumn and stop laying in winter.

A queen is raised from a worker egg, in a cell that is enlarged downward from the comb to look like an acorn. The larva is fed "Royal Jelly" throughout its larval stage. Royal jelly is a milky food with the consistency of yoghurt. It is produced by young worker bees from glands near their mandibles, the movable mouth parts. In contrast the worker larvae are only fed Royal Jelly for the first 3 days, then honey and pollen.

The queen exudes a pheromone called "queen substance", a substance whose chemical formula has been analysed. This is attractive to worker bees, who ingest it by grooming the queen with their tongues. They spread it within the colony by feeding each other - see photograph below. This prevents the workers developing their own ovaries, and so regulates the organisation within the colony.

Swarming

Since bees can only survive in a colony, the only natural way that they can reproduce is to split and send out more colonies. This is called swarming. It takes place in late spring and summer, but swarms have been seen in autumn. In a hive that is about to swarm, the queen stops laying and the bees raise about a dozen queen cells, depending on the strength of the colony. The queen flies off with the swarm, up to half the bees in the hive. Before they leave, they will ingest as much honey as they can from their stores, to tide them over until they have colonised their new hive. The remaining bees will continue to maintain the old hive and tend the brood and the developing queen cells.

When a queen hatches she will seek out other virgin queens and they will fight to the death, using their sting to kill their rivals, either newly hatched queens or those still in their cells. After disposing of her rivals the Virgin Queen will venture out on her mating flights.

- That is what we're told in standard texts. However, in my experience there are many colonies that prevent this royal sororicide. Royal Succession in the hive isn't necessarily as lethal as that practiced by the virgin queens in the courts of the Tudors! In the hive the remaining workers often protect the unhatched queen cells after the Queen Mother has left with the main swarm, and soon after each virgin queen has emerged she will swarm with a retinue of workers, usually far less than in the main swarm – typically up to three thousand. Such a secondary swarm is called a cast, and a hive can lose up to half a dozen casts after the main swarm, leaving few or no bees to keep the hive going.

In the same manner as for the main swarm, a cast will seek a new home and start to build wax cells ready for storing honey and pollen and brood. However the virgin queen will have to mate before she starts laying. Whether she starts her mating flights from the parent hive or the new hive is uncertain. In a prolonged period of bad weather she may not mate within a month, or her mating flights may be limited, so she will have received insufficient semen to build up a strong colony for the winter. A well-mated queen will lay up to a million fertilised eggs during her lifetime, about 5 years. During the height of summer she will lay up to 1000 eggs a day.

Queen surrounded by her retinue of workers.

Before the queens emerge, you may hear 'piping' in the hive: it is the queens who are about to emerge challenging each other. Several days after emergence from her cell she will begin to produce queen secretions and be recognised by the workers. She will gorge herself on pollen and nectar, then seek out other virgin queens or queen cells, which she will kill (NB only if the workers let her - see above). Mating takes place 5 or 6 days after emergence, she could mate with up to a dozen drones over a period from a day to a week, depending on the weather, then start to lay eggs 2 or 3 days later.

Stages in the development of a Queen:

egg - 3 days; larva - 5.5 days; pupa - 7.5 days total time: 16 days
(Worker : 3, 6, 12 total time: 24 days)

So assuming the colony swarms after the queen cells are capped, it could take up to 7.5 + 6 + 7 + 3 days before before the new queen starts laying. This can be confirmed by the appearance of eggs and young larvae in the central combs. This makes, rounded up, a total of 24 days after the swarm. In bad weather, with delayed mating, add another 10 days. After that, the old colony is unlikely to survive since the queen isn't properly mated. If many casts emerge, it is unlikely that there will be any queen left to take over, with not enough workers. Such a colony will be "swarmed out" unless the beekeeper removes all bar one or two queen cells after the main swarm has left with the old queen.

Supersedure

Sometimes a colony may replace its queen without swarming. The colony will make queen cells, as though in preparation for swarming, but there will be fewer: typically one to three. See figure below. They will be in the centre of the brood, unlike swarming queen cells that are near the edges. After the new queen has mated, she will start to lay, but the old queen will continue laying. Supersession usually takes place in conditions where a swarm is unlikely to survive, for example in autumn, or where there are insufficient bees. It has the advantage that egg laying is not interrupted. The old queen generally dies before the end of the year, though I have seen three queens in one of my hives: daughter, mother and grandmother.

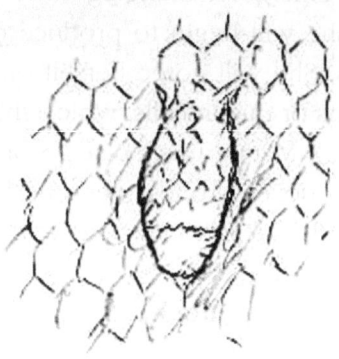

Emergency Queen Cells

If the queen is removed from a hive, the bees soon sense their loss. They select one or two larvae that are less than three days old and raise them as queens, to replace the lost or failed queen. They continue to feed royal jelly to those larvae, and they enlarge their cells to become queen cells. These are called "emergency queen cells", which will eventually hatch to produce virgin queens. One queen will be allowed to emerge to mate, then lay, ensuring the survival of the colony. Usually it takes about 5 weeks after the loss of a queen for a colony to resume raising brood: 14 - 16 days to develop and hatch, 3 days to feed and mature, 7 - 10 days orientation flights, 3 - 14 days for mating flights, depending on the weather. The external indication of a laying queen is the workers bringing in pollen.

If a colony is split, or a nucleus taken, or the old queen is killed for any reason, it will be at least **32** days before a new "emergency" queen starts laying: say **5 weeks**.

What to do about Swarming?

Though swarming is the natural way that bees reproduce, a responsible beekeeper should try to manage a hive in order to prevent:
1. Intrusion on neighbour's land and buildings.
2. Loss of bees.
3. Reduction of the honey crop.

A swarm and any succeeding casts will leave with a high proportion of the bees and honey stores, and there will be a delay until the new queen starts laying. The swarm may not be captured.

There are a number of ways to deal with swarming, but prevention cannot be assured:

a) Regular inspection of the hive during the swarming season and removal of any queen cells that are found. This should be done at 10 day intervals and it has risks: the colony is disturbed and it is difficult to spot all the queen cells, some may be missed and the hive will swarm anyway. I do not recommend it.

b) Clip the Queen's Wing

Some beekeepers find the queen and clip off part of one of her wings. The idea is that if the hive swarms, the queen will not fly far, or will just crawl on the ground so the swarm will cluster near the hive and not be lost. There are problems with this:

Firstly, a risk that the queen may be damaged in clipping her. Secondly, if the colony can't swarm with the clipped queen, it will still raise queen cells and swarm with a virgin queen. The whole colony may abscond. I think queen clipping is cruel and unnatural and ineffective. I do not like it.

c) Replace the Queen

Generally a hive will not swarm if the queen is new and vigorous, for an abundance of her "queen substance" inhibits the workers raising queen cells. So replacing an old queen with a new queen less than a year old is common practice. This is normally done in late summer. It does have a risk, in that the old queen could be difficult to find and the colony may reject the new queen. Because of this, I have never done it, and I do not recommend it unless the colony is very aggressive.

d) Split the Colony

There are a number of ways of splitting a colony, sometimes called "Shook Swarm" or "Artificial Swarm". Well-known methods are Demaree, Pagden, Snelgrove, Horsely. They vary in complexity, but the aim is the same: to separate the queen and a proportion of the flying bees from the colony, so that the queenless bees will raise emergency queen cells. The split hives can later be reunited with only the new queen, or left to increase the stock. The methods I use are explained later in the chapters on brood inspection and propagation.

Drones

The drones are male bees who will fertilise a queen on her mating flight and then die. Drone cells are larger than worker cells and are usually nearer the outside edges of the comb. Typically there are around a hundred drones in a hive during the summer, so only a few manage to mate. At the end of summer, they are ejected from the hive by the worker bees, since there is no longer a need for them. Drone bees are raised from unfertilised eggs, consequently they have the same genes as their mother, unlike the worker bees, whose genes are from one of a dozen or so drones as well as the mother. This is a point to note when attempting to breed desirable traits: good drones flying in a mating area are as important as selecting good queens for propagation.

worker, drone and queen (marked)

Workers

The worker bees are raised from fertilised eggs. They do all the work necessary to maintain the hive and raise the brood of new bees. In an average hive in summer, there are about fifty thousand workers. In summer they live for eight to twelve weeks, but those raised in autumn will survive the winter until spring, when the queen starts laying again. In winter, the population of the hive will dwindle through natural mortality to about twenty thousand bees. They will form a close cluster on the combs in the centre of the hive, huddling together to keep cosy and warm. They gradually consume their stored honey, expending just enough energy to maintain a minimum survivable temperature inside the cluster throughout the cold weather. If they have consumed all their honey, they will starve and the whole colony will die. If the weather is mild and sunny, some bees will fly out for a short period to excrete, remove dead bees and hive debris, then return to the cluster.

Though worker bees are female, in a well regulated hive they are inhibited from egg laying by a pheromone emitted by the queen: "queen substance". This is distributed throughout the hive by mutual grooming and feeding. If the hive is queenless for over two or three months, some worker bees may start laying, but since the eggs are not fertilised they will become drones. Such a hive is doomed to fail.

Detailed studies have found that the glands of workers develop and then atrophy, so that they perform the following duties at progressive stages in their life:

"nursing" – feeding the queen and young larvae with Royal Jelly, and the older larvae with diluted honey or nectar;

"housekeeping" duties – cleaning the cells and the hive;

storing pollen and nectar from the foragers in the combs;

converting nectar into honey by evaporation and adding enzymes;

wax making and comb building;

guarding the hive;

finally, foraging for nectar, pollen, water and propolis.

Despite this progression, they will vary their duties if the circumstances change in the colony, for example to defend against a threat to the hive, or to collect water in a drought. There is no unionised job demarcation in a beehive!

Below is a sketch of part of the brood comb with worker cells occupied by eggs and larvae at different stages of development before the cell is capped with wax. Inside the capped cell a chrysalis forms, in preparation for the miraculous transformation of the pupa into a fully formed insect.

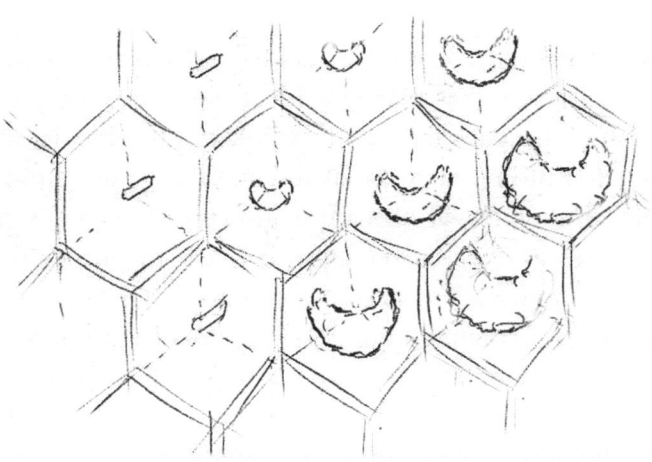

eggs and larvae in worker cells (magnified x 5)

Bees have effective mandibles, which they use to manipulate wax and pollen and clean out old comb or cells in preparation for the queen to lay in, or prior to storing honey or pollen. They are quite capable of biting invading robber bees or wasps, or gripping them before stinging. Dead varroa with bitten carapaces or missing legs have also been observed in the hive debris – see later chapter on varroa resistance.

Pollen and Nectar

Honeybees, unlike wasps, are not carnivorous. They rely on nectar to provide energy in the form of carbohydrates, and pollen to provide protein for growth. Nectar is produced by the nectary of a flower. It consists of water with dissolved sugars, and some aromatic oils.

When there is an abundance of nectar bearing blossom, the bees are active flying in and out of the hive: it is called the 'Honey Flow' or sometimes, more accurately, the 'Nectar Flow'. A nectar flow usually happens in warm weather and is strongest under humid overcast conditions when nectar is slow to evaporate off the flower. You can tell when there is a strong nectar flow by looking at the hive for the following signs:

- bees flying in and out of the hive purposefully, no hanging about, often setting out in the same direction;
- a strong odour of the blossom coming from the hive, accompanied by a loud humming or roaring sound from within the hive. This is caused by the house bees evaporating the nectar to make honey;
- house bees near the hive entrance aligned and fanning into and out of the hive, circulating the air to blow out the evaporated moisture.

Lime, clover, hawthorn, heather, ivy all have distinctive odours. If you look closely at some flowers that bees are foraging for nectar, you may see the bees inserting their tongues through bite holes in the corolla of certain types of flower, to get at the nectar without running the gauntlet of the stamens to transfer pollen. This you will observe in flowers with long corolla, where a honeybee's tongue is not long enough to reach the nectary. Bumble bee's tongues are long enough to do this, so are better pollinators for those types of flowers. Examples are comfrey, runner beans, field beans, and red clover.

Pollen is produced on the anthers of the flower. It is gathered on combs on the worker bees hind legs, which are designed to comb the pollen grains from the anthers of the flowers while they are doing it their tongues are licking the nectary. Some flowers such as the poppy have no nectar, or very little. Then the bees crawl over the anthers in a state of excitement, still combing the pollen directly from the anthers onto their legs. Honey bees and Bumble Bees go mad on poppy pollen, which is black. If you look at the cells in the honeycomb surrounding the brood, you will generally find that each cell has one colour, indicating that the bees segregate each type of pollen. Eg. cells with orange pollen could be dandelion, cells with pink pollen hawthorn etc. The nurse bees pick up the pollen with their mandibles to feed it directly to the larva or to eat it themselves, which they need to do when making Royal Jelly for the young larvae or for Queen cells.

Senses and Communication

The care of bees should take account of the way bees sense their environment and communicate with each other.

Sight

Like all insects, bees see through compound eyes. They can see light of shorter wavelength than we can: into the ultraviolet spectrum, so flowers which may appear to us to have one colour could appear multi-coloured and patterned to bees. They can also sense the direction of the sun from the polarisation of light in the sky, which helps them to navigate when foraging.

Smell and Taste

Bees detect odour through their two antennae, which direct them to flowers with nectar and pollen. They can also detect scents generated by glands in their own bodies, chemical signals called pheromones, which communicate the state within the colony, and alert the colony to threats and actions that should be taken for its well-being: actions such as defending the hive against intruders, raising new queens, deciding to swarm. The hive can sense the presence of a good queen, for the queen herself emits a pheromone called "queen substance" that is carried round the hive from bee to bee and prevents the worker bees from laying eggs. If the hive has an old or failing or missing queen, the bees sense this and act accordingly by raising queen cells from young larvae, to replace the queen.

Sometimes the beekeeper can smell the pheromones given off by the bees, in particular the alarm pheromone, which is said to have the scent of banana oil. That will be a sign for the beekeeper to cease operations and close up the hive! Another distinctive smell is given off when bees wish to indicate the hive entrance to other bees that may be new foragers, unsure of its position. This smell is quite strong when a swarm is taken or when it is first entering the new hive. Bees align themselves with the entrance and lift their tails and fan the pheromone from scent glands in their tails. It is quite a pleasant smell, detectable to the human nose.

The beekeeper should be careful to remove a sting from the skin or cloth as soon as possible, for the sting gland gives off a scent that attracts other angry bees to the spot, thus pressing home the attack. Bees can also detect carbon dioxide, so the beekeeper should avoid breathing into the hive and blowing onto a frame of bees. They hate the scent of beer! Observe hygiene by keeping your equipment and bee suit clean and observe oral hygiene.

Hearing and Touch

Though bees don't hear sound in the air, they can detect vibrations in the hive, including the piping sound made by queens who are on the point of emerging from their cells, and the vibrations made by an excited forager returning to indicate the source of nectar or pollen. The successful forager indicates the direction and proximity of a source of food or water or a potential new location for a swarm by performing a "waggle dance". This was discovered and interpreted by Von Frisch, and it is the only animal language that man can understand.

Magnetism

Experiments have been done to prove that the orientation of bees is affected by the magnetic field, in a manner similar to pigeons and other animals.

Races of Honey Bees

The species name for the honey bee is *Apis Mellifera*. Recent research indicates that it evolved in Africa and from there spread to Asia and Europe.
http://www.sciencedaily.com/releases/2006/10/061025181534.htm

The species evolved into different races in isolated regions, each race adapting to the climate and flora of that region. The main races include:

Italian, Carniolan, Caucasian, North European, African. From these hybrids have been produced, usually due to human intervention: transport to new continents, America and Australia. Beekeepers have been breeding stock that would show desirable characteristics:

Good honey production, hardiness, docility, and reduced tendency to swarm. I would add resistant to varroa and wasp attacks.
http://bees.uark.edu/Keeping/types-of-bees.html
http://en.wikibooks.org/wiki/Beekeeping/Honey_Bee_Races

One of the most sought-after strains has been The Buckfast Bee. This was developed by Brother Adam of the Buckfast Abbey community in Devon. He was a German monk (born 1898) who was in charge of the apiary. He developed the strain from bees from many countries, being able to control the breeding programme because the breeding apiary was in an isolated valley in Dartmoor.

My own breeding programme since 2000 has been far cruder: it is based on survival of the fittest, the fittest strains being those colonies that thrived despite the attacks of varroa, adverse modern agricultural practices and dreadful weather. They have come from local swarms, usually those that entered my empty hives: I reason that such colonies have already shown resistance to varroa, having come from buildings and hollows that have not been treated by beekeepers.

Those colonies that thrive I split, those colonies that are aggressive or unproductive I merge: multiply the good, suppress the bad. My best colonies are uniformly black, docile and productive, with a tendency to supersede the Queen rather than swarm. I took this picture on 4th March 2014 of bees gathering nectar and pollen on my winter honeysuckle. You can see the different colouring of the bees – The one in the foreground is black on each segment of the abdomen, the other is orange on the top two segments. It is said that the native British bee was black, but was wiped out by the Isle of Wight disease, Acarine (tracheal mites) around 1900. In at least 2 of my hives the bees are uniformly black, but in the others they have varied colours. You would normally expect variation within a hive, since a well-mated Queen would have the semen of about a dozen drones.

Bees on Winter Honeysuckle

The winter of 2012 –13 and the following early spring saw a 50% mortality of colonies in the UK. Some beekeepers imported colonies to restore their stock, but I and many other Beekeepers disapprove of importing bees for a number of reasons:
a) Possible introduction of disease and alien creatures such as the Hive Beetle
b) contamination of the local genetic pool, which has evolved to the local conditions.

I see the high mortality of 2012-13 as beneficial: the fit strains survived and the unfit strains died. The surviving colonies have less competition for forage. The problem in the UK, and I suspect Europe and America as well, is not lack of bees. It is lack of foraging: nectar and pollinating flora and an environment not polluted by chemicals.

A Year in the Hive

In climates where honeybees live: Mediterranean, desert, temperate, mountain, subtropical, the colony will adapt to the weather and the state of the local flora. For example, in a desert region when nectar and pollen are abundant after rain the colony will build up stores and increase in numbers of bees. During drought it will feed on its stores and decrease in numbers. This chapter describes what happens inside a hive in a temperate climate, left to nature: that is, the lifecycle of a hive without human intervention.

Winter

In winter in a temperate climate the population of the hive is at its lowest, normally between 10,000 and 20,000 worker bees and a Queen. In the middle of winter, during a cold spell, the bees cluster on the honeycombs inside the hive. The cluster is in the form of a ball of bees, intersected by the honeycombs as described in the previous chapter. Depending on the number of bees in the hive the cluster will be between 5 to 10 inches diameter (12 to 25 cm). The bees consume their stored honey and generate heat by quivering their wing muscles. As the stores of honey are consumed, the cluster migrates upward through the combs. Bees on the outside of the cluster bite through the wax capping the comb to get at the honey, gradually being overtaken by bees in the centre so they take it in turns to form the outside layer. The queen will stay warm in the centre, and will have stopped laying since autumn.

Should you look into the top of the hive on a cold day you may see bees at the top of the cluster, some with their heads in the cells of honeycomb. Their abdomens will be pulsing and their wings quivering as they metabolise the energy of the honey to maintain the temperature of the cluster. Of course you should only open the top of the hive in winter if you have reason to believe that its stores are depleted and you need to put a block of fondant above the cluster as an emergency feed.

During a spell of mild weather, bees will fly out to defecate, which they will not do inside the hive unless there is an outbreak of dysentery. Poor quality honey or fermenting honey, combined with prolonged periods of bitter cold, will increase the likelihood of dysentery, which will spread rapidly in the hive and kill the colony.

Spring

As the days get longer, the queen will start to lay, only a few eggs each day and gradually increase laying as the days get longer. As well as flying out to defecate, foraging bees will start to bring in pollen and nectar from early flowers. The young bees will gradually replace the over-wintered bees as they die.

This is the time of highest stress on the colony, for the workers are now feeding the Queen and young larvae, requiring a lot of royal jelly. They also have to raise and maintain the brood temperature at 35 degrees centigrade, and should the weather turn bitterly cold at this time, the cluster may have to contract to keep the centre warm. The larvae in cells on the outside of the cluster will chill and die, so there may not be enough young bees raised to replace the over-wintered bees. If there was insufficient honey left from winter, and a lack of nectar bearing flowers and blossom, the colony will starve. This is also the time when a weak colony is vulnerable to nosema, amoeba and dysentery.

During the period from late spring to summer, a well-founded colony will build up its numbers to around fifty thousand or more bees, depending on the weather and availability of forage. On the outer edges of the cluster, where the cells in the honeycomb are larger, the Queen will lay unfertilised eggs. These will develop into drones, that fly well away from the hive on warm days in summer to congregate in mating districts, where they await the arrival of virgin Queens.

Summer

In nature, bees reproduce and multiply by swarming. Not all hives will swarm, though, for a number of reasons, usually because the colony has insufficient bees, due to:
a) bees dying in winter or spring from disease, stress or starvation;
b) a failing Queen, old or not well mated, so insufficient egg laying and new bees to build up the colony;
c) the colony came from a late swarm or a small swarm, and was unable to build up its strength.

Even a strong colony may decide not to swarm, for swarming is always a risk. The swarm may not find a suitable home, a cavity of the right volume that can protect it against weather and which it can defend. If the swarm manages to occupy a new hive, it may be too late to build up enough stores of honey and pollen to overwinter. The new Queen in the swarmed hive may not mate properly because of bad weather and lack of drones. Instead of swarming, the hive may replace its Queen by supersedure, as described in the previous chapter.

Autumn or Fall

As summer ends, the Queen will reduce her rate of laying and the drones will be ejected from the hive. This is a crucial time for the colony to build up its stores of honey and pollen, to sustain it through winter and into the spring. Often, a colony with an old or failing Queen will raise another by supersedure, so not all drones will be kicked out, especially if they drifted in from other colonies.

And so into winter, the cycle repeats.

The Artificial Hive

Men still collect honey from wild colonies in jungle trees or from cliffs and caves, risking death from being stung and falling, but since ancient times bees have been kept for their honey, wax and other products, hived in all manner of receptacles: clay pots or pipes as in ancient Egypt, or hollow logs suspended above the ground, which is still done in Kenya.

Skep Hives

In Europe, hives were made of coiled straw bound with split willow, woven into the shape of a deep pudding bowl and called "skeps". They were placed upside down on a flat surface, with an open shelter to protect them from rain but allow the bees to fly freely. The bees made comb that stuck to the inner wall of the skep, and so was difficult to remove without disturbing or killing the bees and cutting it out.

I remember seeing skep hives with removable straw heads in the folk museum in Celle, North Germany. In late summer the hives were put out to forage the heather on Lüneburg Heath, and the heads placed on top, to be filled by the bees with new comb of heather honey. The removal of the head when full of honey was relatively easy. It was cut off and any bees inside were smoked out. To identify the owner of each skep, or just for fun, heads were fashioned in various shapes to represent hats, noses and ears.

Skep hives on the heather

Modern Hives

The modern hive has removable frames, an invention of an American clergyman, L. Langstroth. He discovered the idea of "Bee Space", the distance between surfaces inside a hive which the bees will leave clear of wax and propolis: between 6 – 9 mm. This enables the honeycombs to be mounted within wooden frames, which can be easily removed for inspection or rearranged in the hive, since the bees will generally only build comb on a plane within the frame. There are many types of modern hive that have removable frames, including the Langstroth, the Dadant, the British National Hive and the WBC, invented by an Englishman, William Broughton Carr (WBC) and the design published in 1890, some time after Langstroth. They all have the same basic design.

The Nucleus

The nucleus is a small hive that can hold up to 4 or 5 frames. It can be used to hive a small swarm or cast, or to raise a new colony by taking some frames of brood and stores and bees from a strong hive to increase the stock.

Top Bar Hives

Today there is a body of beekeepers who are trying to reproduce the natural hive structures that bees make when not constrained by artificial hives. These hives are without frames, but use top bars that the bees are meant to attach comb to. Two popular types are the Warré Hive and the Horizontal Top Bar (HTB) Hive.

The Warré Hive

The Warré Hive was developed by Abbé Émile Warré (1867-1951) for the purpose of simple, economical beekeeping. It has square chambers, on top of each chamber rest horizontal wooden bars. The bees are meant to build comb to hang from each bar. The top chamber is the first to be occupied when a swarm is captured. As the colony thrives and fills the top chamber with comb, brood and honey, a second chamber with top bars is put below it and the colony gradually builds more comb and works its way down into the lower chamber. Then another chamber with top bars is put below that and so on. Eventually the top chamber will be filled with honeycomb and can be cut off and the honey extracted.

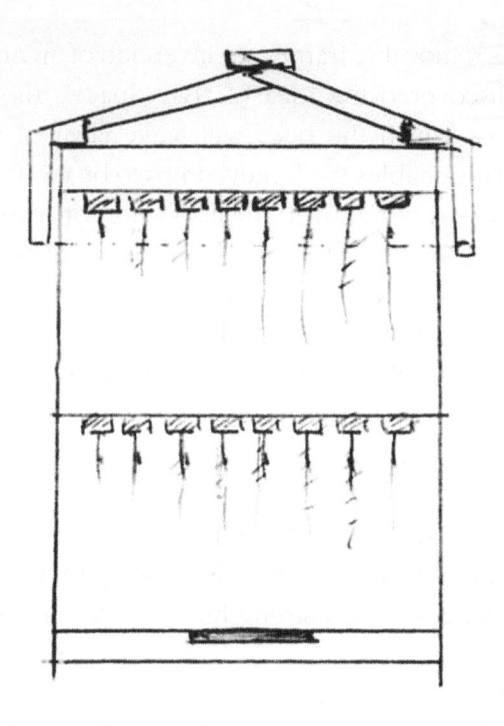

Schematic diagram of a Warré hive with 2 chambers.

This shows the hive with a floor, a narrow entrance, two brood chambers or boxes, a top section (called quilt), and a ridged roof.

The inner dimensions for each chamber are 30 cm square and 21 cm high. Top bars rest on rebated ledges at the top of each chamber. There should be a gap between the top bars of at least 0.5 cm to allow bees to move above and below the top bars. There are 8 top bars for each chamber.

Details of construction can be found on many web sites devoted to Natural Beekeeping. One such is http://Warré.biobees.com/plans.htm

There are some points regarding the construction and use of the hive as described in that article that I will comment on:

Improvement

1. Instead of a top quilt box and top bar cover cloth, I use a crown board: a square frame with plywood that has a hole in the middle – the feed hole. The reason is that it is easier to see the state of the hive through the activity and density of bees immediately below the crown board. A good indication can be seen just by looking through the feed hole, without lifting the board and disturbing the bees.
2. A flat wooden roof covered by a waterproof material such as galvanized iron sheet or polyvinyl flooring is better than a ridged roof, since it can be

upended on the ground and used to rest upper boxes that are taken off in order to inspect lower boxes.
3. Despite putting the hive in a sheltered spot, it may need guy ropes to stop it toppling in the storms that are becoming more common.

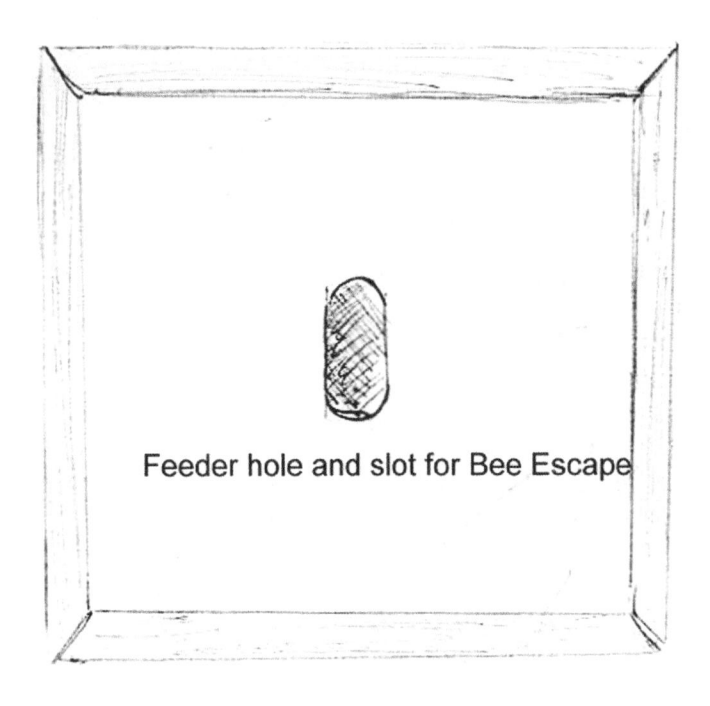

Feeder hole and slot for Bee Escape

crown board

Simplification
1. Use a flat floor without legs and stand the hive on a pair of concrete breezeblocks. It will be more secure, not prone to damp and wood rot, and take a greater weight.

The Horizontal Top Bar Hive
The Horizontal Top Bar Hive is a long horizontal trough with a triangular cross section fixed to a stand or suspended from the branch of a tree to protect it from ground predators. It has top bars resting transversely across its length and a covering roof that can be lifted off. The intention of the triangular cross section is to allow the bees to build their own comb as they hang in a chain, without the constraint of an oblong frame. The colony expands along the length of the trough by building comb from the central top bars outward to the adjacent bars as they are added by the beekeeper. Honey is taken by removing outer bars of capped honeycomb. This hive is usually about 2m long, and can be divided

into 2 or 3 sections separated by vertical boards. Each section will need its own entrance, usually several wine-cork sized holes drilled at the ends or on the sloping sides of the trough.

Details of construction can be found on many web sites devoted to Natural Beekeeping. One such is http://aabees.org/ebooks/how_to_build_a_top_bar_hive.pdf

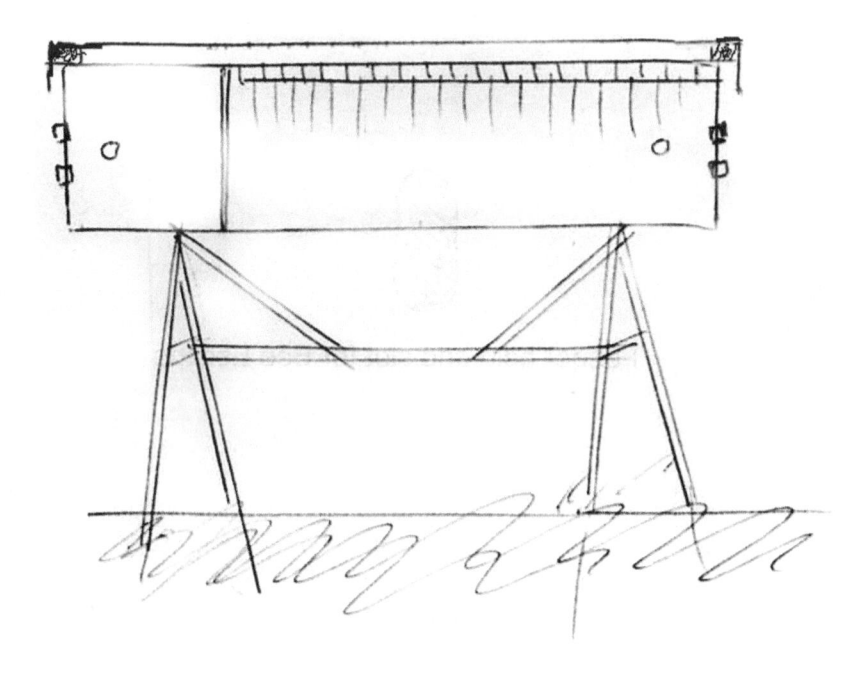

Schematic Diagram of Horizontal Top Bar Hive

Caution
1. Be careful when you buy Top Bar Hives. A number of new beekeepers I know have purchased poor quality hives and been disappointed: the roofs have leaked, the top bars badly fitting and chambers distorted. Purchase your hive from a carpenter who is an experienced beekeeper and keeps his own bees in his own made hives.
2. As for conventional frame hives, place your hive in a spot sheltered from wind, not prone to flooding, isolated from large animals and human traffic. These hives are more vulnerable to being blown over than conventional hives.

Pros and Cons of Warré and HTB

This chapter gives some points in favour and against top bar hives, in comparison with conventional frame hives. It then compares the advantages and disadvantages of the Warré and HTB hives. It is not intended to be comprehensive or definite, since your choice of hive will depend on your own capabilities and experience, and perhaps what is available.

Since the bees build all the comb themselves in top bar hives and skeps, you do not need to buy wax foundation. Foundation is a thin sheet of wax embossed in a honeycomb pattern that is fitted inside the frames of a conventional hive. The bees build their cells on the foundation. The advantage of using frames with foundation is that the bees need to make less wax, but I think this is not much of an advantage, since the bees' own comb is so thin and economical of wax. The advantage of not using foundation is that wax used to make it comes from many sources. Though it is sterilised to kill diseases and fungus, it still has any chemicals that the other beekeepers who supplied the wax may have used.

The disadvantage of top bars compared with frames is that you have to be very careful to hold the honeycomb so that it hangs vertically from the bar, otherwise it will easily break off the bar. Though my approach is to only inspect the combs when necessary, handling of combs will be required if diseases such as foulbrood are suspected.

It is easy to expand the HTB by moving the partition sideways and putting new top bars in the gap. This can be done easily without disturbing the brood cluster. Expansion with the Warré requires a new box to be placed underneath, called "nadiring". This involves lifting the entire hive off its floor and placing the new box with top bars on the floor, then lowering the rest of the hive on top. If the hive is already heavy with honey, it will require at least two people to do it: one to lift the hive, the other to place the new box underneath. If you put the new box on top instead of underneath, called "supering", then it is much easier and can be done by one person. That method is used with conventional frame hives.

The advantage of adding a new box below is that the brood cluster will migrate downward and occupy new comb. Conventional beekeepers replace old brood comb after a few years to avoid the build up of fungal spores in old comb. With nadiring, the brood will occupy newly made comb. The disadvantage of nadiring is that the top of the hive will be filled with honey, and the honeycomb that is removed as part of the honey crop will have comb that was formerly occupied by brood, with chrysalis cases embedded in it. Therefore it cannot be eaten as comb honey: the honey will need to be extracted by uncapping and spinning, or cutting off and straining.

One advantage of the Warré hive is that the top bars can be replaced by frames of the right size, since the walls are vertical. In theory triangular frames could be used in HTB hives, but in both cases it defeats the object of letting the bees build natural comb unconstrained by a frame. Some Natural Beekeepers believe that unframed comb transmits vibrations better within the hive, vibrations that are made by successful foragers, other workers or challenging queens, a form of communication within the hive. However, it doesn't explain why bees ignore this theory and extend the comb to fix it to the wall of a hive, which I have observed in different types of hive including hives without frames.

Skep Hives

Skep hives are the traditional form of hive, made of a spiral of straw woven with split cane or willow to form a domed container. In the skep hive the comb is attached to the inside wall of the skep, so it can only be inspected by looking up from beneath, or by turning the skep upside down – both operations quite disruptive. A long handle dentist's mirror and a torch could be used to look at the comb in detail.

Of course there is no way of splitting skep hives for swarm control. However for harvesting surplus honey, the top cap of the skep (if there is one), can be removed during the nectar flow and an empty container or small skep can be put over it. In the case of the Sun Hive, a box with wider spaced top bars. During a strong honey flow, the top combs will be full of capped honey, and the Queen will not go through it into the top chamber: it is a 'honey barrier'. The bees will build comb upwards from the top of the skep into the chamber above, so a layer of bars for the bees to build upwards from will enable the combs to be removed when they are full of capped honey.

Sun Hive

A variant of the skep pattern is the Sun Hive, which is becoming popular amongst Natural Beekeepers. It is made of bound straw as the conventional Skep Hive and covered in cow manure for insulation. Unlike the Skep Hive it is egg shaped, with a dome that can be removed, and the bottom half is pointed with a fan entrance at the bottom. This is to match the natural catenary shape of the honeycomb, and maintain a bee space between the wall of the hive and the comb. There are parallel arches under the dome, from which the bees build comb downward into the hive cavity. There is a circular hole on top of the dome, with a wooden cover that can be removed during a honey flow and covered with a small box ('gift box'), which the bees can fill with honeycomb.

The Sun Hive can be inspected by taking off the dome and lifting each arch with its attached comb, or inspected from below. The combs cannot be interchanged, since the dimensions of each arch and the comb beneath differ in order to fit snugly under the dome and within the lower part of the hive, leaving the "bee space" separation from the wall of the hive.

Starting Beekeeping

The best advice to those who would start keeping bees is to join your local beekeeping association. Though the majority of beekeepers in National Associations use frame hives, some members of your local association may have top bar hives. In the UK there is an organisation of Natural Beekeepers of whom the majority keep top bar hives: Warré, HTB, Skeps or Sun Hives. In joining a local branch you will be able to observe expert beekeepers in action and benefit from their advice. Other benefits from joining the association are:

- Savings through sharing expensive equipment such as honey spinners and wax extractors.
- A source of bees from swarms and nucleus, far cheaper than buying from commercial suppliers.
- Instruction and assistance in handling bees.
- Insurance for your hives.
- Belonging to a friendly community of people with a common interest.

Safety Precautions

Use common sense! For example, don't place a hive where people or large animals frequently pass by, or next to a neighbour's garden. Don't open the hive when people are likely to be nearby.

- Only open up a hive on a warm day, when bees are flying in and out of the hive in large numbers. There will be less disturbance and cooling of brood.
- Ensure that your bee suit has no gaps. In particular, that there is no gap between your gloves and the sleeve, and the trousers are firmly tucked into the top of your rubber boots. The veil or mask in front of your face should have no holes and it should not touch your skin.
- Use well-fitting rubber gloves, either standard household gloves, or if you are confident that the bees are relatively docile, disposable surgical gloves, which will be more hygienic for the bees. I would not recommend the leather gloves with canvas sleeves, sold by beekeeping suppliers, since they make delicate handling difficult. Clumsy handling upsets the bees, and the leather doesn't stop the sting penetrating to your flesh: in fact it often provokes stinging.
- The smoker should be charged with cardboard or sacking and well lit.
- Your hive tool or knife should be on hand. I prefer a stainless steel table knife because it does less damage to the woodwork of the hive and frames.
- Before opening, always give several puffs of smoke to the hive entrance, then lift the roof and give a few puffs over the top.

- Have a clear plan of what you intend to do: the manipulations that will be performed and equipment that may be needed.
- Don't run a petrol mower or strimmer near the hive.

Essential Equipment

1. Hive and hive parts.
2. Bee suit: the essential item is a veil, a fine black mesh that covers the face and is fitted at the top to a hood or a hat, and at the bottom to a jacket or a boiler suit. They are usually white, to keep the wearer cool and indicate cleanliness. To complete the outfit, wear Wellington boots and thin marigold or disposable gloves.
3. Smoker: a tin container with a hinged funnel on top and a side tube to admit puffs of air from attached bellows. This is filled with corrugated cardboard rolled into a cylinder, which is lit. By squeezing the bellows, air is puffed into the container and it emits smoke through the funnel, which is directed into the hive to pacify the bees.
4. Hive tool: a piece of flattened metal about 10 inches long and an inch wide, with a sharp straight chisel at one end and a bent scraper at the other. I find the Hive Tool unwieldy and prefer to use a stainless steel table knife because it is safer and it doesn't damage the wood of the hive or the frames through chiselling.
5. Honey extracting equipment: expensive equipment is not needed if you are a "Natural" beekeeper using top-bar hives, or are just taking honey off a few frames. In that case, cut the honeycomb off the frame or top bar into a kitchen colander, chop it to break the cells of honey and strain it through a fine mesh.

Collecting the Hive

Often retiring beekeepers advertise their hives in local papers, sometimes with equipment such as smokers, extractors and spare hive parts. The best time to collect a hive is in early spring, when the bees have consumed most of their stores and the hive is light. Do this in the evening or in cold weather, when all the bees are in the hive and not flying. You may need to use a wheelbarrow or trolley to carry the hive from its stand in the apiary to the transporting vehicle. To prevent bees escaping, stuff a damp rag or sponge into the hive entrance. In the case of a Warré, make sure that the floor, boxes and roof are stuck together. This will usually be the case, since bees stick together any adjoining parts of the hive with propolis, an aromatic resin that the bees make from various plant materials. It has antiseptic and anti-fungal properties. The bees apply it to gaps and crevices in the hive to protect the colony from draught and damp. To be doubly sure that the hive will not come apart during the move, bind the hive from top to bottom with a tight strap band.

If the hive is heavy, get someone to help lift it. Don't forget to bring the hive stand, unless you have already set up a stand in the new apiary. Take the hive to the new apiary and place it securely on its new stand. Finally remove the cloth or sponge from the hive entrance. It is advisable to wear your bee suit, gloves and rubber boots when lifting the hive from the old position and placing it in the new position. Don't forget to open up the hive entrance after you have placed it on its stand!

The best place for a hive is a plot sheltered from wind and not liable to flooding, without any overhanging branches that may break off and hit the hive. If there are any adjoining fields or paddocks, fence off the hive area with the hive more than 7 feet (2m) away from the fence, so that livestock cannot get too close and knock it over. Place the hive with the entrance facing away from footpaths and ideally facing a hedge or wall that will make the bees fly up and above the heads of livestock or people. It is a good idea to place a sheet of impenetrable material such as corrugated iron or carpet on the ground in front of the hive to suppress undergrowth, which could obstruct the bees' flight to and from the hive entrance.

Most of the operations on top bar hives have their counterpart in the conventional frame hive, but in Top Bar hives the bees are allowed to manage their own organisation of hive space, to build comb without the constraints of frames or queen excluders. A problem with top bar hives is that the bees do not always follow the lines of the bars, and they may build comb at an angle that traverses several bars. If that happens the bars cannot be removed separately should the combs need to be inspected for brood diseases. Nor can outside bars be easily removed to get the honey, in the case of the Horizontal Top Bar Hive. To encourage a captured swarm to build comb along the top bars, put a line of wax along the lower edge of each bar, so they can use that as a starter for comb building. It may work, but bees don't always do what they're told!

Setting up a Top Bar Hive: Hiving a Swarm

Generally a new Top Bar Hive will be first populated with a swarm rather than transferring bees from a nucleus or another hive, which is easy with a conventional frame hive.

The bars should be positioned with the same spacing between each bar as the brood frames in frame hives: 1.44 inch (3.7 cm), which will be the separation between the centres of each comb. The bees should be encouraged to build their comb along the line of each bar, down from the centre. This can be done either by shaping the bottom of the bar as a ridge, or by slotting a thin strip of wood or cardboard down the centre. A light coating of beeswax will prompt the bees to build nice parallel comb down the centre of each bar – see figures 1 – 3.

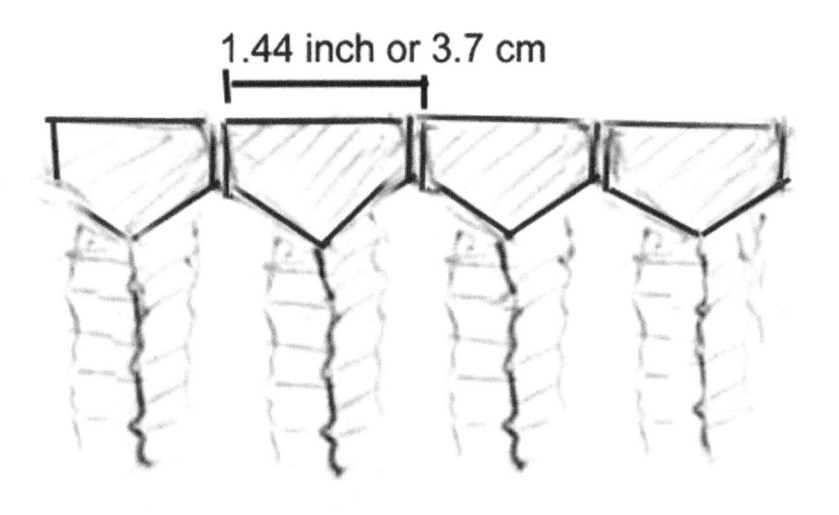

fig. 1 end on view of HTB bars and comb

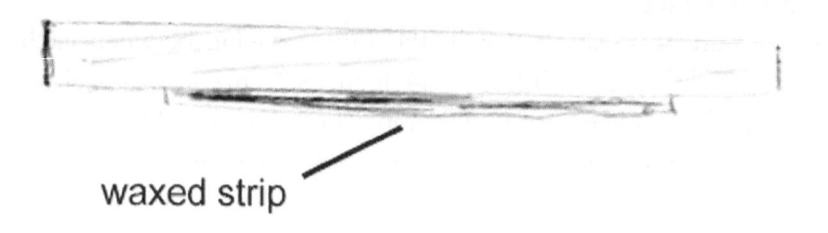

fig. 2 starter strip under bar

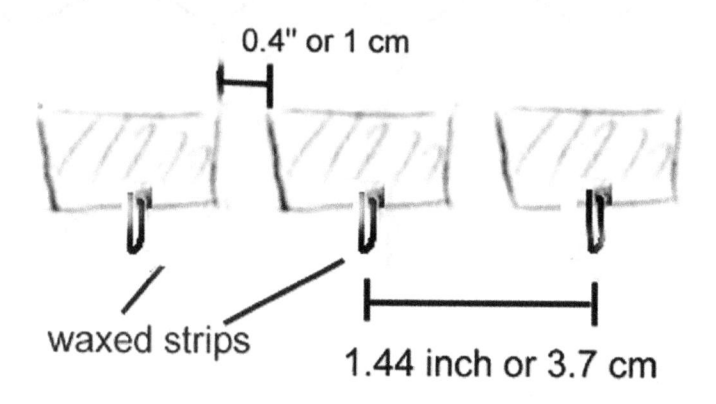

fig. 3 top bars for Warré

In the Warré Hive the bars are narrower, leaving a 0.4 inch (1cm) slot for the bees to move up or down between chambers, as in the frame hive. In the HTB there is generally no space between the bars, which could be a problem if any bees are left above them when the roof is replaced. If the bars are fitted below the rim of the trough, a long plywood sheet with feed or ventilation holes could be used as a cover, and this would not be a problem. Care should be taken that there are no gaps under the roof that would admit invading bees or wasps.

A swarm can be introduced into the hive in the same way as for framed hives. It is easy to walk the bees up a ramp to the entrance of a Warré Hive, but difficult for an HTB. It is probably best to drop the swarm in from the top, having first removed several bars until they have settled inside.

The configuration of the brood will be different between the Warré, and the HTB. I use the term "brood cluster" to mean the combs that contain cells with brood: eggs, larva, capped pupae, nurse bees and adjacent pollen and honey. This pattern of combs should not be disrupted, since it gives the necessary warmth and protection for the development of the brood.

When the swarm takes possession of the hive, it will start to build comb as described in the chapter "Lifecycle of the Honeybee". If it does what the beekeeper intends, it will extend the comb down from each top bar, making parallel combs, and start to fill them with nectar, honey and pollen. In a prime swarm the old queen will start egg laying within a day or so, and the brood cluster will rapidly expand downward as the combs are extended and new combs started on adjacent bars.

In the HTB, downward expansion is limited to the depth of the trough, so the colony expands the brood by starting new combs on adjacent bars.

In the Warré, the general practice is to put another chamber underneath, with a set of top bars. This is called "nadiring", as distinct from "supering", where the chamber is put on top. As the colony fills the top chamber, it will start to extend downwards by starting new comb on the bars of the lower chamber.

Eventually the colony will reach a point of equilibrium where the rate of egg laying by the queen matches the rate of hatching of the brood. During this time the number of bees in the colony will have increased, and the foragers will be producing a surplus of honey, with which they will fill the comb at the top and sides of the brood cluster. See figures 4 – 5.

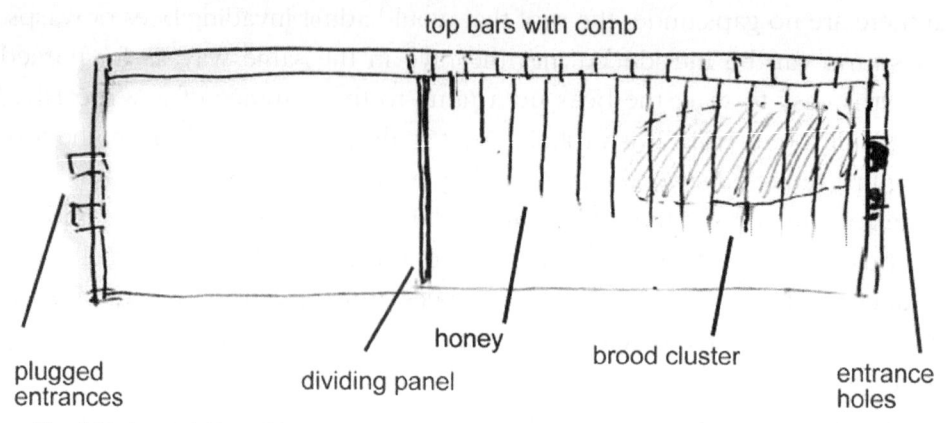

Fig. 4 Horizontal Top Bar Hive

Note the dividing panel, which can be moved along to make more space as the colony expands, or can be used to split a strong colony in order to control swarming or make increase. The entrance holes are made at both ends of the hive, but plugged at the end that is not yet occupied. Alternative entrance holes are often made in the sides of the hive. The number of open entrance holes should be adjusted depending on the strength of the colony, and restricted in autumn and winter to prevent incursion by wasps and mice and to reduce draughts.

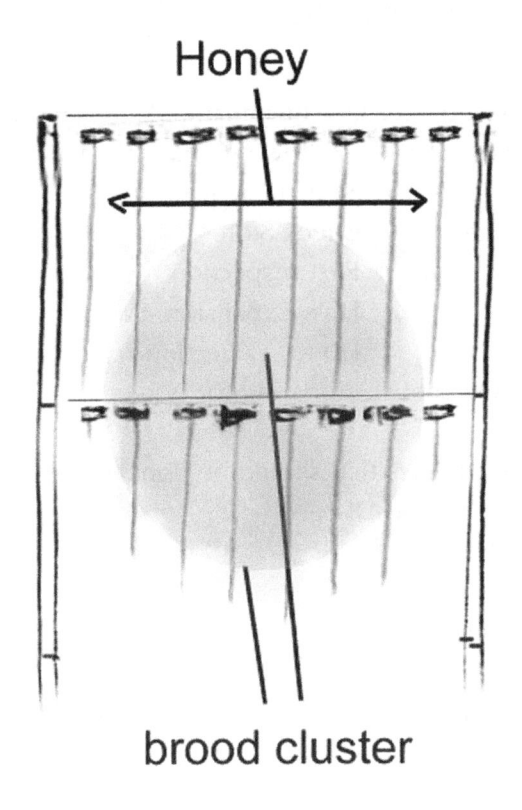

Fig. 5 Warré Hive

This shows 2 tiers of a Warré hive. Note that here the brood cluster has descended and occupies the middle of the hive.

Seasonal Activities

In keeping with my aim to reduce hive manipulations to the minimum essential for productive beekeeping, the following timetable is a guide to managing the hive throughout the season. The main activities are:

January – March:	Check Stores
April – May:	First Inspection
June – July:	Hive Expansion, Swarms
July/August:	Honey Collection
September/October:	Preparing for Winter

Other important activities that should be done as the need arises include:
Inspection for Brood Diseases
Emergency Feeding
Swarm Collection
Defence against Pests

The months indicated may vary, depending on the weather and local climate. They are for a temperate maritime climate in the Northern hemisphere, so for the Southern Hemisphere add six months. Like the weather, bees are unpredictable, and the timing of operations will depend on the state of the hive as well as the seasonal weather and location. The months are indicated as a guide, not a hard and fast timetable, so the beekeeper must be observant and alert to the state of the hive and the weather, and act accordingly.

In the following chapters I will explain how the annual cycle of beekeeping operations are applied to Top Bar Hives, in particular the Warré Hive and the Horizontal Top Bar Hive (HTB). In general, these hives are favoured by the Natural Beekeepers, whose aim is to promote sustainable beekeeping and ensure the long-term health of the honeybee.
See:
http://biobees.com/ and
http://naturalbeekeepingtrust.org/

I agree in general with their aims, but some of the methods of keeping bees that I describe in this book, such as propagation and taking honey, may be disputed by some Natural Beekeepers, who keep bees just for the purposes of conservation. It is argued that such human intervention interferes with the natural lifecycle of the colony.

Check Stores

A good beekeeper should have left enough honey in the hive for the bees to over-winter, but sometimes the winter is prolonged, with unusually bitter spring weather as experienced in Northern Europe in 1962-3, and lately in 2012-13. In that case, it is better to feed the bees than allow them to starve. Assuming your hive was collected in winter or early spring, the first thing to do is to check whether there is enough honey left in the combs above the clustered bees. If there is not, the bees are in danger of starvation. The amount of honey stored in the hive can be checked by weighing the hive, but that is a difficult operation, so a fair estimate can be made by tilting it slightly from behind. Be careful not to topple it!

Warré

Weighing the hive can only give a rough estimation, and a better way to check is to take off the hive roof and look through the feed hole in the crown board (or quilt). Do this on a cold day or towards dusk, when the bees are not flying, and be sure to wear your bee hat with the veil fastened. In a Warré hive you should be able to see capped honeycomb on one or two of the frames near the feed hole: you can confirm this by probing with a length of stiff wire to check for capped honey. Poke the wire into the honeycomb and check that honey sticks to the tip. Be careful not to disturb any bees that may be clustering up to the feed hole.

If you are still unsure about the depth of honey, then place a block of the fondant over the central feeder hole in the crown board, or on the top bars under the quilt. If the bees have consumed nearly all the honey at the top of the hive, they will take down sugar from the fondant. See the chapter "Winter Starvation" for more details.

Fondant for feeding bees can be purchased, or you can make it by boiling a quarter pint (0.1 litre) of water, adding 2kg white granulated sugar. Heat to 114 degrees C until all the sugar is nearly dissolved. Then let it cool and stir in a teaspoonful of icing sugar and pour it into flexible plastic containers to set. Some recipes add a small quantity of glucose to make the fondant pliable, but it should be stiff enough not to flow down between the honeycombs.

Far better than fondant is set honey that you may have collected from that same hive in the previous season. Do not feed them honey purchased from shops or other beekeepers, for it may be infected with foulbrood, fungal spores, nosema and chemicals and antibiotics used to treat varroa and other diseases.

HTB

Direct checking of honeycomb above the cluster cannot be done with an HTB without shifting some bars away from the side, possibly disturbing the cluster, so only do this if you are nearly certain that stores are critically low. If you have done this, close up the top bars but leave a gap of 0.5cm or ¼ inch between two bars near the edge of the cluster and put a strip of fondant on the bars over the gap.

Inspection

You can see the state of a hive without opening it and disturbing the brood by observing the entrance and the flight of the bees. Then lift off the roof and look at the top of the crown board (or below the quilt). This can be done with minimum disturbance and little use of smoke. The conditions that you should find in good weather are as follows:

Bees flying strongly, bringing in pollen –

All is well. Lift the roof and apply some smoke.

HTB

Move the partition away from the combs. If bees are crowded and waxing on the end comb, then put in some more bars next to it and close up the partition. If you are short of space you could consider dividing the hive to raise a new colony, or removing bars with fully capped honeycomb. These operations are described later.

Warré
Check the top of the crown board (quilt). If you can glimpse new white wax through the feeder hole, then puff some smoke over it and lift the crown board. If there is a lot of new white wax on top of the bars and the bees are crowded, then you could consider putting another box with top bars in the bottom of the hive (nadiring) or on top (supering), or taking off some honey. These operations are described later.

Few bees bringing in pollen, weak or dying bees
After the initial appraisal of the state of the hive described above, you may find it necessary to do a more detailed inspection if the bees are not flying strongly, or there are weak or dying bees near the hive entrance. This could be due to a number of adverse conditions or disease, which are described in later chapters. It could be because of a weak or failing queen and associated problems such as chalk brood or sacbrood, diseases which are quite common, or foulbrood. Suspected foulbrood should be reported immediately to your local bee inspector, it is a statutory requirement. This will involve opening the hive to inspect the brood combs. Inspection for disease is described later.

The manipulations that are relatively easy with conventional framed hives, such as inspecting for brood disease, queen cells, changing comb, and taking nuclei, are risky with top bar hives. This is because the comb is not held in a frame and can easily break off the top bar. Always hold the comb in a vertical plane and don't twist the bar otherwise it will break off.

The Swarm Dilemma
Not all beekeepers agree with swarm prevention, since it interferes with the natural process of reproduction of the colony. However, you may judge that it is politic to control swarming if you have neighbours who may object to swarms landing in their property. One way to avoid this is to provide an empty bait hive as far as possible within 300 m of the hive, or at known swarm locations. Swarms often favour particular trees, hedges, posts or walls, that may still retain the scent of earlier swarms. See later chapter on swarm collecting. However there is no certainty that the swarm will enter the bait hive, and it may instead occupy a neighbour's building.

Another approach, the one I advocate, is to cooperate with the bee's desire to propagate in a way that doesn't harm the colony. I believe you should do this, even though there is still no certainty that a swarm won't happen at a time when you are absent and cannot do anything about it. The following methods can be tried.

a) Provide more space

See the earlier chapters on the Queen and swarms. Swarming will usually happen with a vigorous hive where the queen is more than 2 years old, or in a hive which runs out of space, either because of rapid expansion of the brood, or because it is full to overflowing with honey. So the simplest approach to swarm prevention is to add more space. With the Warré Hive, the standard practice is to put a new chamber with top bars at the bottom, allowing the bees to build new comb below the brood for the queen to lay in. If there is a strong flow of nectar into the hive (the 'Honey Flow'), I would put a box on top: see below.

With the HTB, additional top bars are inserted next to the brood cluster. Just add one or two at a time, to give the colony time to adjust to the extra space and build new comb on the inserted bars. The dividing panel will be moved to provide more room for the additional top bars. New bars are inserted between the honeycomb and the brood, on which the bees will build new comb, provided there is a good nectar flow and the weather is warm. Depending on the time of year and the weather and foraging conditions, for a vigorous hive you may need to take off honeycomb in order to provide more space and reduce the likelihood of swarming.

At the beginning of this book is a remarkable photograph taken by Sarah Ellis showing what happened to one hive where there was a strong honey flow and insufficient space provided. In spring a jar of granulated ivy honey was placed over the feed hole. The bees emptied it, taking the honey down into the brood chamber, then in summer the colony grew and the bees could only expand by filling first the empty jar with honeycomb, then overflowing and filling the space over the crown board with their artistic creation of beautiful honeycomb!

b) Split the Colony

This is swarm pre-emption rather than suppression, and it isn't always successful. It should only be done if the hive is vigorous, with the brood cluster occupying two chambers in the case of the Warré, or over a dozen combs in the case of the HTB. You must also check that drones are flying in the vicinity, since there is always a risk that you may harm or kill the queen when you open up the brood chamber. If that happens, then the bees will raise some emergency queen cells, but if this is done too early in the season, before drones have hatched, then the new queen will not be mated and the colony will die. There should also be a substantial amount of honey in the hive.

For the **Warré**, the top chamber is separated from the bottom. It is placed on a new stand nearby with a new floor and roof. The queen could be in either hive, and the flying bees will stay with the parent hive.

After about ten days, check the bees flying into each hive, to see which one they are bringing pollen in to. That hive will have the old queen. If it is the parent hive, then swap its position with the new queenless hive, so that the majority of flying bees will support the queenless hive and help in raising a new queen.

With the **HTB** just insert a partition in the middle of the brood cluster and open both ends of the hive, so that bees from the separated cluster have their own entrance at the other end of the hive. As for the split Warré, the flying bees should be directed to the queenless partition, if necessary by turning the hive through 180 degrees in a horizontal plane.

Failure to raise a queen

Sometimes a split hive or a nucleus may fail to raise an emergency queen cell. It may be that the parent queen is so vigorous that there is still plenty of the queen pheromone inside the queenless hive and the worker bees do not recognise their loss of a queen. Always check the parent hive and the offshoot hive (nucleus) to see if one or more emergency queen cells have been raised. If not, take a comb with eggs and young brood from the hive with the queen, and put it in the middle of the queenless hive or nucleus. By then, the bees will have sensed that they are queenless and will raise one or more emergency queen cells on the inserted comb.

Taking Some Honey

Some Natural Beekeepers do not agree with taking honey from the hive, and consider it to be a form of exploitation. I agree that taking so much honey that the bees have to be fed sugar syrup in autumn is bad for the bees, since sugar is not as good for them as their own honey, which contains some pollen and essential oils and some vitamins. However I argue that the main reason for keeping bees is for their honey. Honeybees are needed for pollination services only in areas where there are large areas of monocultural crops, such as oil seed rape in the UK, and almond orchards in the USA. There, the environment is degraded by the use of herbicides, pesticides and chemical fertilizers to such an extent as to eliminate the natural pollinating insects such as bumblebees, ants, butterflies and hoverflies. The presence of beehives adds to the pressure on the native insect pollinators, and many ecologists consider that relying on honeybees to pollinate these crops risks total crop failure should the hive bees die off, as is increasingly likely with such ills as colony collapse disorder and other diseases: such use of honeybees is truly exploitative. See the article by Hillary Rosner in Scientific American, September 2013, "Return of the Natives".

So the only justification for keeping bees is for the honey they provide. Keeping them for any other purpose, or for no purpose at all, is contrary to the principles of biodiversity and ecology, considering that honeybees are alien to all the continents except Africa.

If there is plenty of capped honeycomb and the hive is running out of space, then the beekeeper may judge it prudent to remove some as a honey crop. This should only be done if there are enough combs of honey left in the hive to ensure the bees have sufficient for their needs, and it will depend on the weather and time of the year. Normally the end of July is best, but some localities will have a surplus of honey from spring blossom or rape, or in August and September from heather or Himalayan Balsam, Aster or Goldenrod.

On no account should honey be taken from comb that is part of, or adjacent to the brood cluster.

a) Honey from the HTB Hive

To take the honey, use smoke if necessary to quieten the bees before opening the hive. Lift the outside honey combs in turn, only taking those that are fully capped. Take a handful of long grass leaves and gently wipe any bees off the comb and down into the hive. The reason for using grass instead of the traditional goose feather to brush the bees off comb is because feathers will pick up some honey or nectar from uncapped cells, which will stick to the bees and harm them. But if the grass becomes sticky, it can be left inside the hive above the quilt or crown board for the bees to lick off the honey, and a new handful of grass used. So no honey or bees will be wasted.

When free of bees place the honeycomb into a suitable container with a loose cover, such as a sheet of polythene. Try to avoid breaking the comb, otherwise robbing may occur. Of course you have to be extra careful with comb on top bars, since the weight of the honey could easily break it off the bar. Leave at least 27 lb (12 kg) of honey for the colony to over winter: about 5 or 6 full combs.

b) Honey from the Warré Hive

During a honey flow the bees in a strong colony build honeycomb above and at the sides of the brood chamber, if there is space. If the standard operation of the Warré hive is followed, the brood cluster will move down into the lower chambers as they fill the top chambers with honey. Honey can be taken off, but there should be enough honey left for the bees to continue unchecked in raising brood, and most importantly to survive winter and spring until the next summer's nectar flow. In practice, this means there should be at least two chambers at the top of the hive that are full of honey before you consider taking off any honey. The top chamber should be full of capped honeycomb, with no brood. The chamber below should contain at least 27 lb (12 kg) of honey, and left on the hive. The top chamber should be inspected before you decide to remove the honey, to make sure that none of the combs contain brood. Even if the queen has started to lay in the lower chambers, the colony will tend to fill the outside combs with honey and extend the brood combs down the middle from the top chamber, so that the brood occupies two or even 3 chambers, in 3 or 4 deep combs which are waxed onto the intervening top bars without interruption. If this has not happened and the bees have behaved as intended, the honeycomb can be removed.

Taking honey from a Warré in this manner will disrupt the colony, since you could be lifting active brood. Even if the brood is lower down the hive, the comb will have been brood comb, so the cells will be lined with chrysalis walls. That comb cannot be eaten whole, which you can do with new honeycomb, so you will have to spin out the honey, or press or scrape it off the comb.

I recommend that you super the hive after it has filled 2 or 3 chambers, by putting another shallow chamber on top, with empty shallow frames, and a sheet of newspaper below. The shallow chamber should be half the height of a standard box. The frames should be placed directly above the top bars of the chamber below, with a "bee space" gap between the top bars and the bottom of the frames. The frames should be wide enough to restrict the gaps between them to a "bee space", between 6.35 mm and 9.53 mm, so that the bees don't build comb between the top bars and the frames, or between the frames. That is, the honeycomb should be framed, as for supers in frame hives. A queen excluder may be used, but will probably not be needed if the tops of the combs in the top chamber are all full of capped honey, since the queen is unlikely to ascend through a layer of honey – sometimes called the "honey barrier". The capped honey frames may be removed one at a time, using a handful of long grass to gently brush the bees off the comb.

If top chambers are removed for honey in the traditional Warré method, much of the honey would come from cells that were formerly occupied by brood and pollen. This cannot be eaten as honeycomb, and must be extracted by uncapping. I would much prefer honey from new cells built with new wax, which do not contain old chrysalis and pollen, so follow my recommendation! In the wild, bees tend to build their comb for storing surplus honey away from the entrance, making combs with larger cells. So for a Warré, you should provide space at the top of the hive for the bees to store new honeycomb.

Extracting the Honey

Do this in a bee-proof room: an outhouse, utility room or garage. Ideally there should be a high window in the room, to which any bees that have remained in the supers will fly and you can open it and let them out. But make sure you close it again, otherwise you will be invaded by bees seeking to recover their honey! If using the kitchen, it is a good idea to spread a large sheet of polythene on the floor before you start, to collect any spilt wax or drops of honey.

Comb honey

If you have followed my advice with regard to supering the Warré hive rather than nadiring, and adding new top bars for the bees to make new honeycomb, then you need not do the following for spinning honey out of the comb. Instead, lay the comb flat on a wire grille and cut out oblongs of fully capped comb and put them into 8 or 12 oz. plastic containers with clear lids. See picture below.

If you can avoid breaking the comb off the top bar, then you can return the top bar with its unused comb to the hive whence it came. The bees will recover honey from uncapped comb that remains attached, and may even refill the gaps with new wax.

Honeycomb

Comb honey is much sought after and will command a higher price since the flavour of comb honey is far more intense than that of extracted honey, because the essential oils and distinctive flavours are locked into each individual cell. It is perfect for eating on brown bread toast, since the wax (which is good for the stomach) will be ingested with the toast and not stick in the teeth.

Though extracted honey in jars is a delicious product, comb honey retains the aromatic compounds and flavour within the capped cells. Some of this is lost in the extraction process of uncapping. My advice is to go for comb honey rather than extraction and bottling. It is faster and cheaper and you get a more valuable product.

If you have a Warré hive and followed the traditional Warré method of nadiring rather than using supers, the honeycomb will have been used for brood. So it will have the chrysalis cases embedded in it, and it cannot be eaten as comb honey. Therefore you will need to extract the liquid honey, either by uncapping it and letting it drip out, or by centrifuging it in a spinner. One advantage of doing it this way is that the central sheet of wax in the honeycomb will remain intact if you handle it carefully, and it can be put back in the hive and will save the bees the effort of making new comb.

If you decide to spin you will need the following equipment, which most local associations can lend to their members, with advice and assistance:

a) Honey Spinner or Extractor
b) Honey Container with a tap, on top of which is fitted a Honey Strainer fitted with a mesh that filters out the wax
c) Uncapping Knife: this is a heavy double-edged knife with which to slice the wax off the top of the honeycomb before putting the frame in the spinner. I prefer an ordinary sharp carving knife, since I find the specialised uncapping knife unwieldy and dangerous.

This is what you do:
Take each comb in turn, hold it over the Honey Container with its Strainer on top, then slice through the wax capping on each side of the comb, letting the cappings fall into the strainer. Put the comb in the spinner with one face propped up against the mesh. See figure:

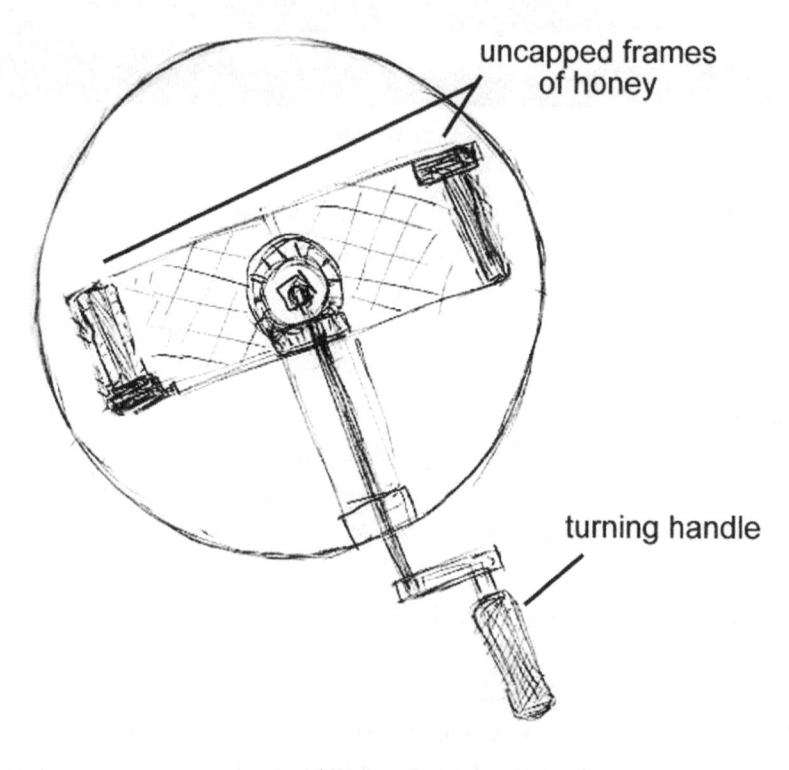

honey spinner

Some spinners will take 2 combs, others 3 and 4. Try to ensure that the combs are roughly the same weight, to balance. At first, turn the spinner gently until most of the honey has spun out from one side of the combs. Then lift the combs and turn them round so the other sides are propped against the mesh, and spin again. When most of the honey has spun out, turn the spinner faster for a minute or so, then lift and turn the combs again and give a fast final spin. The reason for the initial gentle spinning is to avoid the comb breaking under the weight of the centrifugal force on the honey.

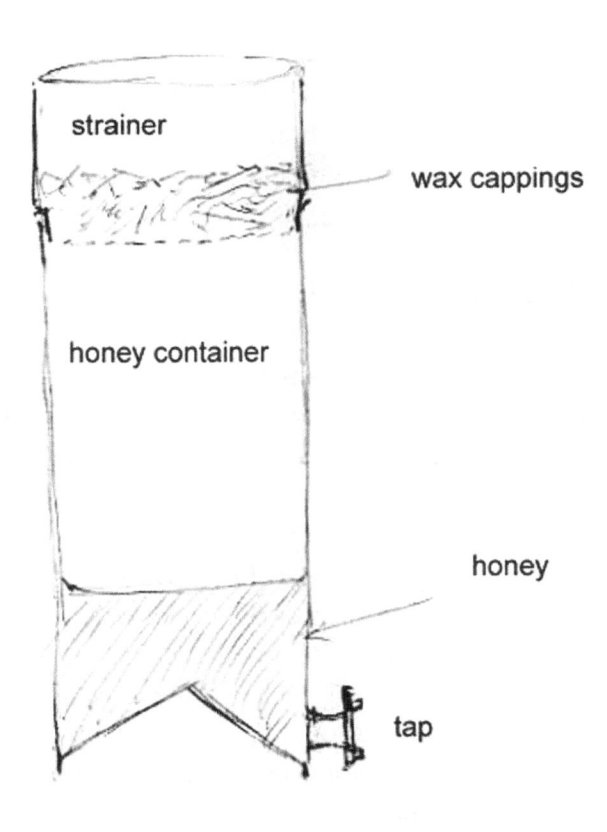

honey strainer and settling tank

When you have spun the honey out of the combs, put them back in the hive so that the bees can recover the honey still left in them. When you have finished spinning, or when the honey in the spinner has reached the level of the combs' top bar (which will retard any further spinning), lift the spinner onto a bench and put the Honey container with its strainer under the tap of the spinner and open the tap of the spinner, so that the honey flows out of the spinner and through the strainer into the container below. Make sure the tap of the container is closed tight! Leave them for at least 12 hours for the honey to drain out of the spinner, through the strainer and wax cappings, and let it settle in the container. Then it can be tapped off into your honey jars.

The wax cappings contain a fair amount of honey even after they have drained. This can be separated by melting the cappings gently in an oven, in the same way that honey that is set in the comb such as ivy or oil seed rape honey – see below. Do not mix this with the honey that you have tapped off already, since its flavour, though quite palatable, will not be as fine as the unheated honey.

There may be a strong flow of honey in August if your hive is near heather, or in September and October from ivy flowers. In both cases, it is unlikely that you can spin out that honey. Heather honey is a gel, and the combs must be pressed to squeeze out the honey. Ivy honey sets hard and I leave it for the bees to consume during winter.

Honey crystallised in the comb

Sometimes the honey has granulated in the comb and cannot be extracted by spinning. This happens if the hive over-wintered with a super and the frames contain ivy honey from the previous year or if there is a nearby field of early flowering oil seed rape, which tends to granulate early. The granulated honey can only be recovered by melting the comb in a pan in the oven at a low temperature, about 85 degrees centigrade. After about 90 minutes, the comb will have melted. Let it cool for about an hour and the wax will set on the top of the pan. Make a hole in the wax at opposite sides of the pan and pour out the honey into jars. Put the wax into a sealed container for rendering later – see wax production. Ivy honey will mellow after a year or so and can be blended with other types of liquid honey to make excellent creamed honey. Both heather and ivy honey have distinctive flavours, which are highly prized by some, but are not to everyone's taste.

Composition of honey

Honey is a clear liquid when first bottled. It consists mainly of sugars that have been processed by the bees from the nectar, to form a combination of fructose and glucose. There are also traces of the aromatic compounds that come from the flowers that the bees have been foraging on, which give various types of honey their distinct flavours. The bees have evaporated most of the water off the nectar to concentrate the sugar and convert it from fructose. They add enzymes that help preserve the honey and inhibit fermentation. Ripe honey should have less than 20% water before the bees cap it, which makes it viscous at room temperature. Indeed, one of the criteria for judging honey is high viscosity and density.

The colour of liquid honey can vary from a pale parchment, through amber of different shades, to a dark treacle colour. Most liquid honey will crystallise after a few months and become opaque set honey. See the photograph below of examples of the various forms that honey takes. Crystallised honey (jar on the left) can be melted if you place the jar in a pan of warm water, 80 deg. C, but be careful to remove it from the heat as soon as it has melted, usually after an hour, for it will lose much of its nature and flavour.

Crystallised honey has a tendency to ferment after a year, especially if it has not been filtered to remove grains of pollen and wax. You can use this to make mead (honey wine), or if you intend to keep this honey, it is best to melt it on a gentle heat as described above. Skim off any bubbles and waxy debris that rises to the top and put the lid back on.

Different forms of honey

In whatever form or colour your honey appears, you can be happy that it is truly organic, provided that you have not used chemicals, nor fed the bees with sugar or other man-made substances, and have used only wax from your own chemical free hives as foundation.

This is an example of what can be achieved by a healthy hive, even during a season of appalling weather that the UK experienced in the summer of 2012. In the wettest and coldest June on record, the brood chamber was covered with a sheet of newspaper. Above it was placed the queen excluder and a super of foundation, and above that the crown board and roof. During a short period of nine sunny days in July, the only decent weather during the whole summer, the super was rapidly filled with honeycomb, fully capped with beautiful white wax – see photograph below.

From this I extracted and jarred 32 pounds (14.5 kg) of delicious clear honey, very pale: mainly Himalayan balsam with some bramble - see sample of 3 below. It won first prize in the Pale Liquid Honey class in the Division's annual show.

part of the 2012 honey crop in 1lb jars

Now this colony of bees was a small swarm that I caught in Bruton in July 2011, the year before: hardly enough bees to fill a pint pot. It was almost certainly a cast from a colony of feral bees that occupied a disused old chimney for over 12 years. I hived it in a nucleus box and in August fed it sugar syrup and pasteurised apple juice (some that I'd set aside from my cider making) and it grew rapidly. I transferred it to a National brood box, where it built up on ivy nectar and pollen in late Autumn. It was over-wintered on an open mesh floor.

In May, which was bitterly cold and wet, there were symptoms of nosema, with bees crawling below the hive entrance. I put a board under the open mesh floor to stop cold air entering from below the brood. I removed the outer frames of old comb, which I suspected contained nosema spores, and covered the inner occupied frames with newspaper, to help the colony maintain warmth in the brood. Despite the wet June, it built up strength to draw out new frames of foundation and occupy all the brood chamber.

I put a tray under the mesh floor for a day, then I examined the debris under a 10x magnifying glass. There were signs of damaged varroa, young and old mites. There were also several white antennae from chrysalids that were removed by the bees from varroa-parasitized cells, indicating varroa sensitive hygienic behaviour.

Wax Extraction

The most efficient wax extractor is a solar melter, which is a box with a double glazed top lid and inside it an open melting pan, such as an old baking dish, with a mesh strainer fitted across the middle. On a sunny day, place the solar extractor in the sun and prop it up so it faces the sun and put the cappings and old comb into the pan above the strainer. The wax will melt and run through the strainer and collect at the lower side of the pan. It can be poured into a mould or collected in the evening when it has set. Make sure that the glazed lid of the melter fits well, since bees will be attracted to the smell of the honey in the melting wax.

For large quantities of wax, a steam extractor may be used. This has an electric immersion boiler on top of which sits a stainless steel container with another perforated stainless steel container fitted inside it. The wax cappings are put into the perforated container. The steam melts the wax and leaves a residue of old brood cells and pollen pellets in the perforated container. The molten wax flows out through a tube, to be collected in a suitable vessel. Your best plan is to borrow a steam wax extractor from your local association.

Uses of Beeswax

Beeswax is a valuable material. It was used for church candles, burning with a bright steady flame and not guttering and smoking like tallow. It is also used for furniture polish, giving a pleasant aroma to the wood, and for strengthening button thread. It is also an efficient waterproof for cloth. Beeswax that has been pressed into sheets embossed with a honeycomb pattern are used in frame hives as foundation, which the bees draw out into comb for brood or honey. I only use my own beeswax, knowing that it is free of insecticides and other chemicals.

Preparing for Winter

Make sure that the hive is secure against wind and flooding. Also secure against invasion by wasps and mice – see Hive Pests.

If you have been greedy and taken too much honey off the hive, you should feed it - see Emergency Feeding.

Ventilation

In winter, many colonies succumb to damp rather than cold, because poor ventilation will allow mould and fungal infections to develop inside the hive. This is less likely if a mesh floor is used instead of a board floor, but some may be worried about very cold winds causing a draught in the hive and chilling the colony. Some crown boards (quilts) have a series of holes near the edges to allow ventilation, or you could put matchsticks below the corners of the crown board.

Unplanned Activities

These are activities that are not part of the seasonal cycle but are nonetheless important if you wish to be a responsible beekeeper.

Emergency Feeding

As said previously, I would not need to feed a well-established hive, preferring instead to leave enough honey for its own use and to maintain the strength of the colony until the next season's honey flow. However it may be necessary to feed a new colony that needs to build up for winter, for example if it is a late swarm and you don't want to lose it.

Spring Feeding

The good beekeeper will have left enough honey on the hive for the bees to last until the first spring blossom. If honey was taken off and the hive was still light in Autumn, then it should have been fed sugar syrup in Autumn, to make up sufficient stores for over-wintering: that is, if the bees had enough honey stored for over-wintering, there should be no need for spring feeding. But if the stores are found to be depleted by mid-March, or early April if the spring is wet, spring feeding will be needed to prevent the bees consuming all their stores. The rate of honey consumption will increase rapidly in spring as the queen starts laying and the worker bees feed the brood, and if the weather is bad they will not be able to bring in nectar from early spring blossom, so they must be fed sugar syrup to prevent starvation.

Sugar syrup for spring feeding is prepared by dissolving 1 kilogram of white granulated sugar (cane or beet sugar) in 1 litre of boiling water. I use a 2 or 3 litre plastic paint tub with about 50 holes in the lid. The holes can be made with a dart or small awl, about 1mm or 0.04 inch diameter. The sugar syrup is put in the feeder and allowed to cool.

When you feed the bees, you should wear your bee costume and veil and boots, even though you are not opening up the hive, since the bees may fly at you through the feeder hole in the crown board (or quilt) when you lift off the hive roof. There is no need to smoke, unless the hive is very aggressive. In that case, the queen should be replaced: easier said than done! But late summer or autumn is the time to do it.

Autumn Feeding

A good beekeeper should leave enough honey in the hive for the bees to over winter, without the need to feed sugar syrup. There is no doubt that honey is a superior food, and the growing body of Natural Beekeepers are finding that bees do not suffer from gut ailments such as nosema as much as those fed sugar. However, if by October there is little honey remaining in the hive, which you can tell by weighing (see "Checking Stores"), you will need to feed sugar.

To prepare the autumn feed, put a measure of granulated white sugar, either cane or beet sugar, into a container. For every 2 kilogram of sugar boil about one litre of water and pour it over the sugar and stir it until all the sugar is dissolved. When it has cooled, take it to the apiary with a feeder and an empty super or two (depending on the height of the feeder). The sugar syrup for autumn feeding is more concentrated than that used for spring feeding, since the later is consumed immediately by the bees for brood rearing, while the autumn sugar will be stored to over-winter and should be more concentrated to avoid fermentation.

Warré

The feeder is put upside down on the crown board (quilt with feed hole), above the central feed hole. If necessary place several thin sticks on the board and under the rim of the tub, to give clearance for the bees to crawl underneath and get to the holes. The tub should be full to the brim before turning upside down, so that a partial vacuum will form at the top of the tub and prevent the syrup leaking out. Put an empty spare box on top of the quilt, to contain the feeder. See diagram.

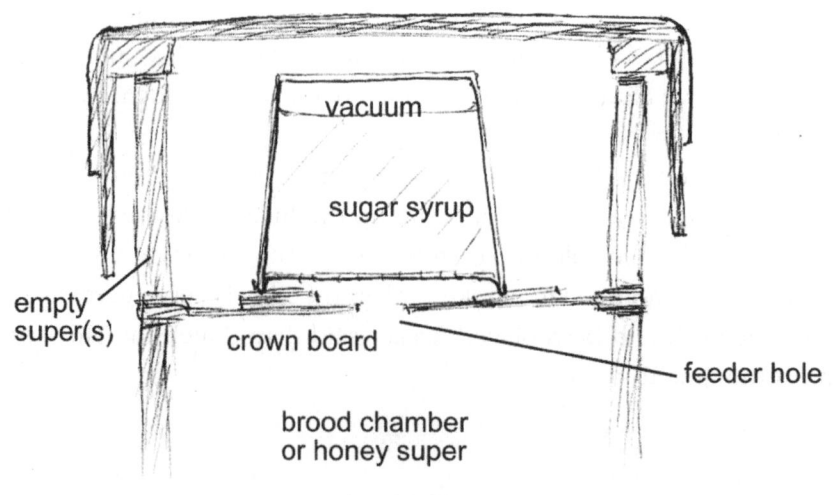

Feeding Warré Hive

HTB

Feeding HTB hives is more difficult to do without disturbing the colony. I would put the feeder in the trough in a side chamber with a partition that has a small gap underneath, so that the bees can get to it from their occupying chamber. An inverted container with perforated lid, or a bowl with straw to prevent the bees drowning are suitable. See figure 6.

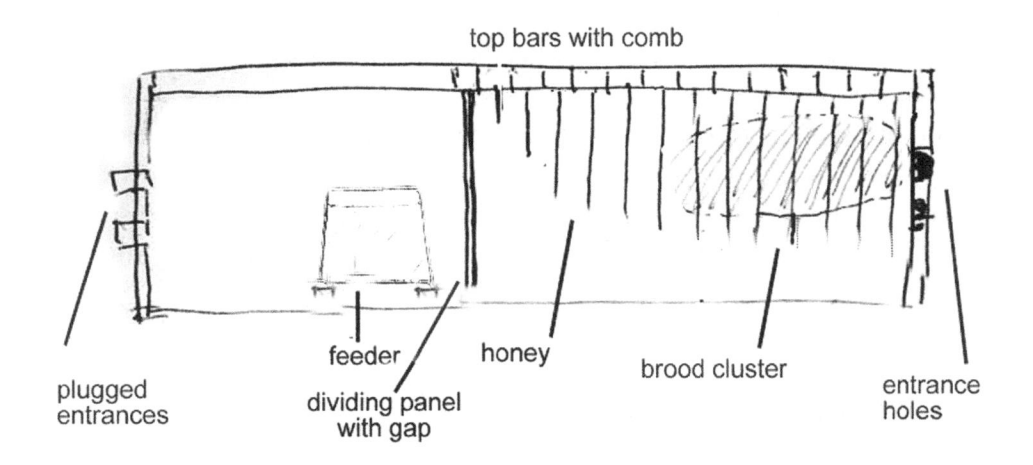

Fig. 6 Feeding HTB

When you feed the bees, you should wear your bee costume and veil and boots, even though you are not opening up the hive, since the bees may fly at you through the feeder hole in the crown board when you lift off the hive roof. There is no need to smoke, unless the hive is very aggressive. Check the feeder after a week or so. The bees should have taken most of the sugar down into the hive. If the weather is poor, they may need feeding again. Beekeepers who wish to split the hive in summer, to raise a nucleus colony, will continue feeding so that the raising of brood is accelerated.

As said at the start of this chapter, feeding your bees is not ideal, but it is better than letting your bees starve. Unnecessary spring feeding will incline the colony to swarm and there is a possibility that an early crop of honey will contain the sugar that was fed to and processed by the bees. Such "honey" should not be sold or given away.

Colonies under Stress - Nosema

In spring and early summer, many hives will be under stress in maintaining the brood temperature when the weather is cold, wet and windy. They will not be able to forage for nectar and pollen, and will be rapidly consuming their winter stores. A common disease that shows around this time is nosema, a fungal disease of the gut that shows symptoms of weak bees crawling on the ground outside the hive entrance, and spots of diarrhoea deposited by the bees on and around the hive.

Beekeepers traditionally treated this by feeding fumidil b in a sugar syrup, but this is now banned in the UK. Besides, I believe that you should treat the cause of the stress, which is the chilling of the brood chamber and the presence of nosema spoors in old comb at the sides of the brood, into which the cluster is expanding as the season progresses. So the following non-chemical treatment should be adopted:

1. Open up the hive to expose the top of the brood chamber and remove all the old dry outer brood combs.
2. Cover the inner combs of brood and clustered bees with a sheet of newspaper, folding it down at both sides to enclose the brood (see diagram). This will help maintain warmth in the brood.
3. Replace the outer combs.
4. If the hive floor is an open varroa mesh, then place a board underneath to stop a draught from beneath.

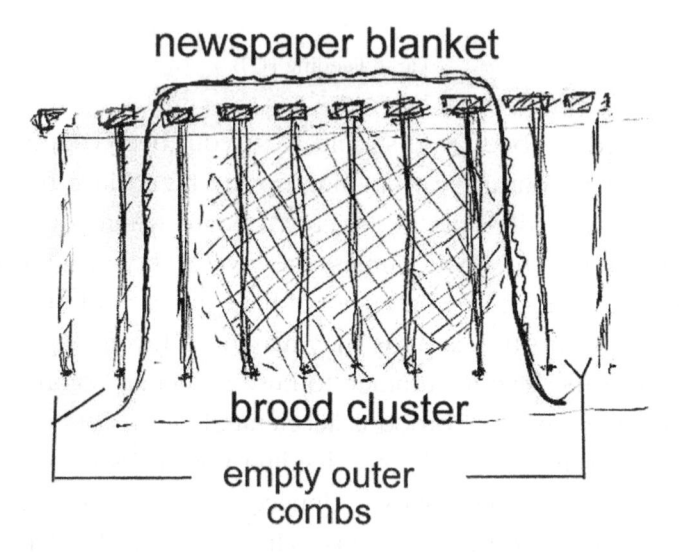

Do the above operation quickly and smoothly, using a minimum of smoke and disturbance of the cluster. Then feed with sugar syrup as for Spring Feeding above. As the colony grows, the bees will gradually bite away the newspaper to expand into the rest of the brood chamber, and as the weather warms up they will clean out old comb and make new.

If you have it, honey from your own hives is much better than sugar. Since it will be part of spring feeding, it should be diluted so that the bees can feed it directly to the brood without having to forage for water. About an equal volume of water should be used. I found the concoction recommended by a Natural Beekeeper to benefit one of my colonies that showed signs of nosema – see Annex 3.

Inspection of Brood

At some stage during the season, frames in the brood chamber may need to be inspected for brood disease. This is a statutory requirement should a government appointed bee inspector need to inspect the hive, or for any reason you suspect the hive has foulbrood (see later), which is a notifiable disease. Top bar hives can be inspected by lifting each bar in turn, but this must be done carefully because there is no frame to support the comb and it can easily break off the bar, which would be disastrous. The comb must always be held vertically and not be turned on its side, since the comb is not supported by a frame (though some Warré beekeepers use frames instead of top bars, for that reason). The combs, especially those holding brood, must be replaced in the same order to maintain the brood pattern.

Since opening up the hive for brood inspection inevitably causes disturbance, you need to have a good reason for opening it. Suspected foulbrood is really the only good reason to delve into the brood of top bar hives. Provided you observe basic hygiene by using clean gloves and not transferring comb and hive components between hives (and particularly between apiaries), the likelihood of foulbrood will be low.

Before you open the hive to inspect the brood, make sure that you have your knife tool and in the case of a Warré, a spare empty brood box. The smoker should be well lit. Grab a handful of long grass to use as a gentle 'bee brush'.

Before opening the hive, puff some smoke in front of the entrance. Don't blow it into the hive, just let it drift in. Take off the roof and put it upside down on the ground beside the hive. Put the empty Warré brood box on the upturned hive roof. Puff some smoke over the crown board (quilt) and lift it off, cutting round the underside of the rim if necessary.

Carefully lift the left side outermost top bar, levering it away from the box using the handle of your knife tool.

Gently brush the bees off the comb into the brood chamber and examine it, then place it in the spare brood box, to remain there temporarily as you go through the rest of the combs in top chamber.

Lever off the next bar and comb from the left. This should be first shifted to the left, so that when lifting it there are no bees trapped between it and the adjacent frame. If combs are lifted directly from their slot, the gap between the adjacent combs on either side is narrow, so bees can be crushed and comb face damaged. See diagram below:

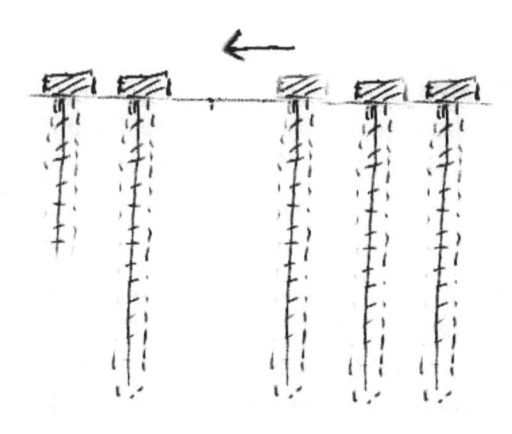

figure: shift before lift

Examine the comb then put it back into the brood chamber, to the left, in the slot that was occupied by the first comb that was removed.

Continue in the same way with the next bar, working from left to right, so that you end up with a vacant slot in the right side of the chamber, then take the first comb from the spare box and put it in the gap left at the outermost right of the chamber.

When you examine each frame you may find the following:
a) capped comb with honey, uncapped comb with honey or nectar or pollen.
b) brood at various stages of development: eggs, larvae, and capped brood, surrounded by cells with pollen, then with honey.
c) comb with queen cells.
d) cells showing signs of disease: chalk brood, sac brood, or Foulbrood (American or European).

Foulbrood is serious and you should notify the Bee Inspector who will confirm and record the disease if there is an infection, and recommend action..

capped brood and stores

In the photograph above, you can see cells of capped brood, where the larvae are now in chrysalid form, surrounded by cells of eggs and larva and pollen. On the top corners are cells with honey, some capped with beeswax.

If the top chamber of the hive contains comb with no brood, only honey or empty, then to continue the inspection you need to look at the chamber underneath. Lift off the top chamber and rest it on the spare brood box at an angle, so that bees are not crushed. Repeat the inspection procedure on the next chamber and so on.

The procedure is much simpler with a HTB: just shift the partition one to the left to make room for the adjacent comb, shift it left and examine it then put it back one place left and so on, moving all the combs one to the left. Put the first comb in the vacant slot at the right.

Swarm Warning

If the brood box is full of bees and they are crowded up to the sides, then there is a possibility of imminent swarming. If you want to make sure that they are on the verge of swarming, then check the brood frames for queen cells. These are acorn sized cells that hang down from the comb – see Figure.

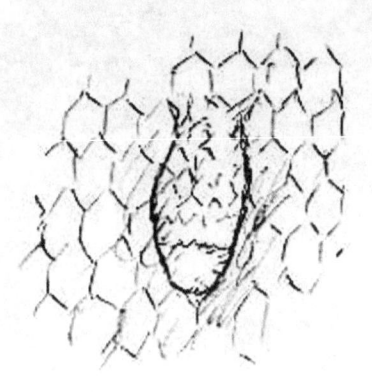

If there are more than 6 queen cells, then the hive is almost certain to swarm, or it has already swarmed. If there is only one or two queen cells and they are near the centre of the brood chamber rather than the outside regions of the comb, then the hive is likely to supersede its queen. That is, a new queen will hatch and the old queen will stay in the hive. The queen mother and her daughter will continue laying eggs until winter when the old queen will usually die. Supersedure is a good thing, for it replaces the old queen with a new queen and you don't lose half your bees and honey production through a swarm.

Before a colony swarms, the old queen will stop laying for a week or so, then leave with the swarm, taking up to half the bees with her. The queen cells will hatch after a fortnight, and the new queens will either fight to the death so that only one remains, or they may fly off, each with a small swarm of about two thousand bees, which is called a cast.

Now the traditional method of preventing a swarm when queen cells have been found is to remove or destroy all the queen cells in the hive. Easier said than done! Almost certainly you will miss some and the hive will swarm anyway. It is far better to split the hive and raise nucleus hives, each with a frame of queen cells.

If the hive has already swarmed (which will be evident by a dozen or so capped queen cells, a reduced complement of bees and lack of eggs in the brood combs), then it is a good idea to remove most of the queen cells in order to prevent possible casts flying off, but leave two queen cells which are still uncapped and have a queen larva with royal jelly. Instead of destroying the surplus queen cells, they could be put into small nuclei with comb and workers, to raise new queens. Mated queens could then be introduced into queenless colonies or used for replacing failing queens.

If no queen cells were seen, but the super is already full of honey, put the additional super with frames of foundation on top of the queen excluder, with the super of honey on top. This will give extra space just above the brood and the young bees will be occupied in drawing out new comb. You may wish to increase your stock later in the season by raising a nucleus, or do selective breeding.

Laying Workers

Since worker bees are female, hatched from fertilised eggs as is the queen, they have the potential to lay eggs. In a hive with a fertile queen, her pheromone "queen substance" inhibits the workers from laying, but in hives where the queen has failed or been absent for several weeks or more, the ovaries of some workers develop and they start to lay eggs. These workers will not have mated, so the larva that hatch from those eggs will be unfertilised and therefore develop into small drones. A colony with laying workers will not raise a queen, even if fertilised eggs or young larvae from another hive are put in it. Nor will they accept a new queen. Such a colony will inevitably fail.

Below is a photograph taken by Joanna Webber of a comb made by a swarm that was hived and built comb on top bars. For some reason the queen was absent – either she went with the swarm as a virgin and failed to return from a mating flight, or she was lost or killed. Some of the cells have rounded tops, others larva and others have many eggs inside each cell, up to half a dozen. Quite different from the diagram of brood comb with single eggs, or the frame of capped brood shown in the photograph at the start of this chapter. In a hive with a fertile queen, cells of worker pupae, larva and single eggs are laid in an orderly concentric pattern.

In recent years there seems to be an increase in the incidences of failing queens, particularly in swarms and nuclei. Some researchers attribute the cause to the use of neonicotinoids in the treatment of seeds of oil seed rape and maize. This and other chemicals are known to affect the navigation of bees, and could account for the queen getting lost in her mating flight. Chemicals used directly in the hive by the beekeeper are also likely to have an adverse effect on the queen.

Laying Workers   photo taken by Joanna Webber 2013

Old or damaged comb

Since old comb is often ignored by the bees and is likely to harbour disease and fungus, it is best removed and new bars put in place for the bees to draw down new comb. The old comb will contain little wax, but it can be recovered in a solar wax extractor or a steam extractor. The old bars should be burnt. If there is some honey in the comb you have removed, then they should be placed flat inside an empty box on top of the crown board (quilt), or in the side chamber in the case of HTB so that the bees can recover the honey. Remove them when they are cleared, after a week or so. The old comb can be cut out of the frame and kept in a sealed container for melting down later and recovering the wax.

Relocating a Hive

If you are taking the hive to a new location, such as heathland or heather hills, then move them after dark when all the bees are in the hive. The hive must be moved at least 3 miles, otherwise the foraging bees will return to the location you moved it from. If the distance is greater than 3 miles, they will settle after a day or so familiarising themselves with their new location.

If during you are relocating the hive within a shorter distance, for example a new spot in your apiary, then you should move it in mid winter during a week of cold weather. If you move it a short distance in any other season, the flying bees will return to the original position, and the hive will be depleted. It probably won't matter if the hive is moved only a short distance, say less than 3 yards, since they will eventually find the new position. If you are moving it more than that distance, then move it to another apiary 3 or more miles away, leave it for a week for the flying bees to get used to their new position and forget their old position, then move it to the new spot in your apiary.

Brood Diseases

There are two brood diseases that are serious and notifiable: American Foulbrood and European Foulbrood. If you suspect that your hive has foulbrood, then contact your area bee inspector to check your hive.

American foulbrood

American foulbrood is suspected if the capping on the brood cells is dark brown and sunken. It is confirmed by poking a matchstick into an infected cell. Instead of a nice healthy grub the cell will contain a sticky brown liquid, which will form a thread when the matchstick is withdrawn. See figure.

American Foulbrood

If the disease is confirmed, the whole hive and its contents including bees and honey, must be destroyed by closing up the hive entrance, pouring a cupful of petrol into it through the crown board and closing down the roof. The bees will be killed within a few minutes. The hive must then be burned in a pit and the ashes buried.

European foulbrood

European Foulbrood is another notifiable brood disease that is endemic in some counties in the UK. It is caused by a bacterium that multiplies in the gut of developing larvae and is spread by the nurse bees who feed the larvae. Its symptoms are a brood pattern with gaps between capped cells, with dying or dead larvae coloured brown or yellow, lying distorted in their cells. Sometimes there is a sour odour present. A serious outbreak can kill off a hive.

If you suspect this disease, call the local bee inspector to confirm it. If the outbreak is serious then the bees and comb should be destroyed, but the hive and its parts can be salvaged by applying a blowtorch to the inside boxes and each frame in turn: scald them but don't burn them. Sometimes the bees will overcome the European foulbrood as the season progresses, if the queen is vigorous and the weather is fine with a good supply of nectar. To prevent cross contamination great care should be taken in transferring combs between hives. Equipment such as gloves and hive tools should be rinsed in washing soda and old comb replaced.

Other common brood diseases

Other brood diseases that are not so serious are chalk brood, where some of the brood cells have a chalky white filling. It is caused by a fungal pathogen and it occurs with weak colonies under stress and damp conditions. A strong colony of hygeinic bees with a vigorous queen will usually overcome this.

Sac brood is a viral disease, where the grub doesn't reach maturity but forms a dry brown sack-like chrysalis lying at the bottom of the cell. These are often a sign of stress in the early part of the season, usually caused by chilling of the brood or nosema and will usually clear themselves in a strong hive with a new queen.

Replacement of old brood comb will help to limit these diseases. I have seen some colonies that will remove old comb by themselves, clearing out the debris from the hive entrance as brown powdery granules and building new clean comb for their brood. These hygeinic bees are often resistant to attack by wasps and varroa..

Varroa

Varroa is a small brown mite that grows to about 1.5mm and feeds on the host bee's blood and lays eggs in the brood cells, preferring the larger drone cells near the edges of the frame. The larvae in an infected cell often hatch with deformed wings, and the varroa mite also spreads viruses such as paralysis within the hive and between hives. It is endemic to Asia, but spread West through Europe during the 1970's. It was introduced into Southern England in 1992 and has devastated honey bee colonies throughout the country. It was first treated with a proprietary chemical such as Bayvarol ™, which was initially successful, but because it was not 100% effective the mites that survived became resistant to that treatment. Other "natural" chemicals have been tried, such as thymol based remedies, but in my experience their aroma is so strong that it disrupts communication within the hive, masking the scent of the regulating pheromones. Non-chemical treatment such as forking out drone cells, or shaking icing sugar over the bees so they would clean off the mites, does reduce the varroa count but at the cost of disturbing the colony.

Hives with a lot of crawling bees near the entrance, or bees with deformed wings, are an obvious indication of varroa infestation. With a bad infestation, you can easily see varroa mites on the floor of the hive, which is why many beekeepers now use a mesh screen to prevent fallen varroa from climbing back into the brood chamber. A sheet of white paper can be placed on the hive floor under the mesh for a few days, then removed and examined. The number of varroa mites that have fallen on the paper indicates the degree of infestation.

Varroa is said to be responsible for the spread of viruses, such as Deformed Wing Virus and others causing paralysis of the adult bees.

Treatment for Varroa

Beekeepers with established hives that have habitually medicated them for varroa may hesitate to suddenly cease medication, fearing that all their colonies will die out. I suggest that a proportion of the hives are selected to start off the chemical free regime, as an insurance against total loss. There are a number of chemical free treatments that can be applied, which are described elsewhere in bee literature and on the Internet. Some of them are:

1. Use of open mesh floor – varroa that fall or knocked off the cluster will fall through the mesh to the ground and not be able to climb back.
2. Another method with the same idea is a bottom board of parallel tubes, invented by the French Beekeeper Marcel Legris.
3. Dust the bees with fine icing sugar. This will prompt the bees to groom each

other, and in doing so remove mature varroa that were clinging to the back of their fellows.
4. Sacrificial drone larva removal. Since varroa tend to prefer the outside drone cells to the central worker cells for depositing their eggs, this will remove the majority of the varroa in their larval stage. The larvae are removed from capped drone cells using a special multi-tined fork. The disadvantage of this approach is that on average a large proportion of drone cells will not have varroa, so the bees' efforts in raising drones will have been in vain. As mentioned above, drones carry the same genes as the queen, and so play an important role in transmitting any inherent varroa resistant traits to the next generation. It could also be argued that drone rearing is a better strategy than queen rearing for improving the strain of bees within an area, so I would not recommend this method.

Signs of Resistance to Varroa

Ron Hoskins, who instigated the Swindon Bee Project, discovered evidence of varroa resistance in his hives after he stopped chemical treatment for varroa. The first signs were bitten varroa in the debris beneath the varroa screen, then later white pupal antennae, showing that the bees were able to detect and remove varroa infected pupae. See the Swindon Bee Project: http://www.moraybeedinosaurs.co.uk/stanton_park.html

You too can check whether your hives have resistance to varroa.

Use a varroa screen as the hive floor. Put a panel of white or bright yellow plastic below the varroa screen, or else a panel with a sheet of white paper. This will catch the debris that falls from the hive and through the screen. Leave the panel in place for 24 hours, then carefully remove it and place it and the debris that may have fallen on it into a clean plastic or paper bag, so that the debris is not blown away. Take it indoors and empty the debris onto a sheet of white paper. Using a hand lens, preferably illuminated x 10 magnification, examine the debris for fallen mites and other items of interest.

You may find pollen, small particles of old comb, white flakes of new wax (indicating that some young bees are producing it from their wax glands), and varroa mites. Look at these mites under the magnifying glass. You will find that some are alive and are crawling. Others may be dead and damaged: bitten bodies or legs removed. You can confirm this using a microscope. See photographs below, which I took using an illuminated magnifying lens, x 10.

You may also find white antennae, which are from larvae that have been removed from their cells before hatching. These are signs that the colony has developed a resistance to varroa, by hygienic behaviour. Not only that, the bees can also recognise and remove infected larvae from their cells. This is a good development and ought to be encouraged by selective breeding. It is happening in parts of England and it is noticeable that some feral (wild) colonies are managing to survive for years and even produce swarms. Such swarms are valuable, and all my colonies have come from them.

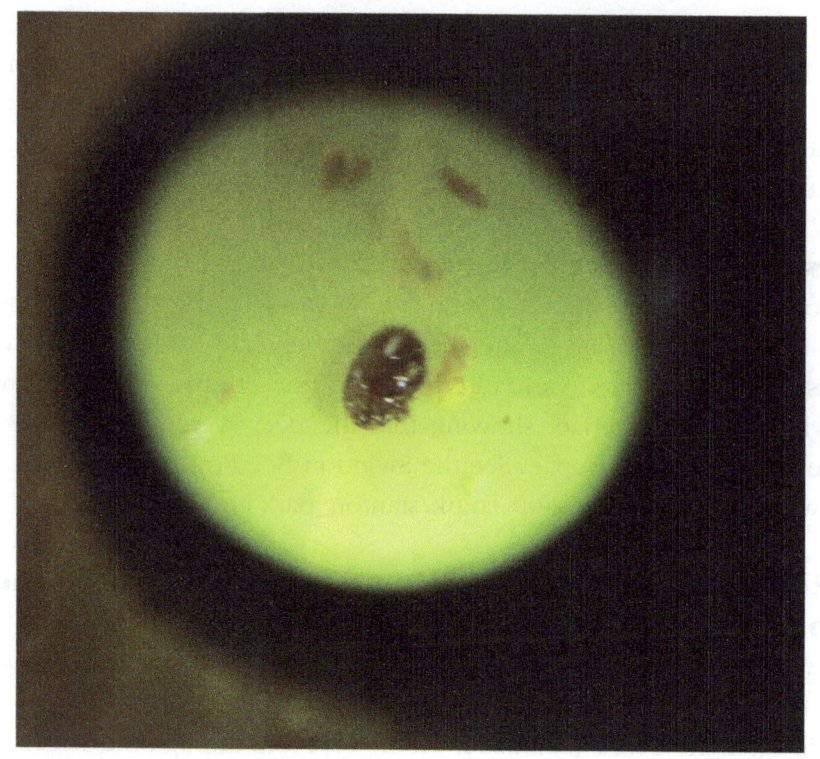

Varroa bitten by varroa resistant bees

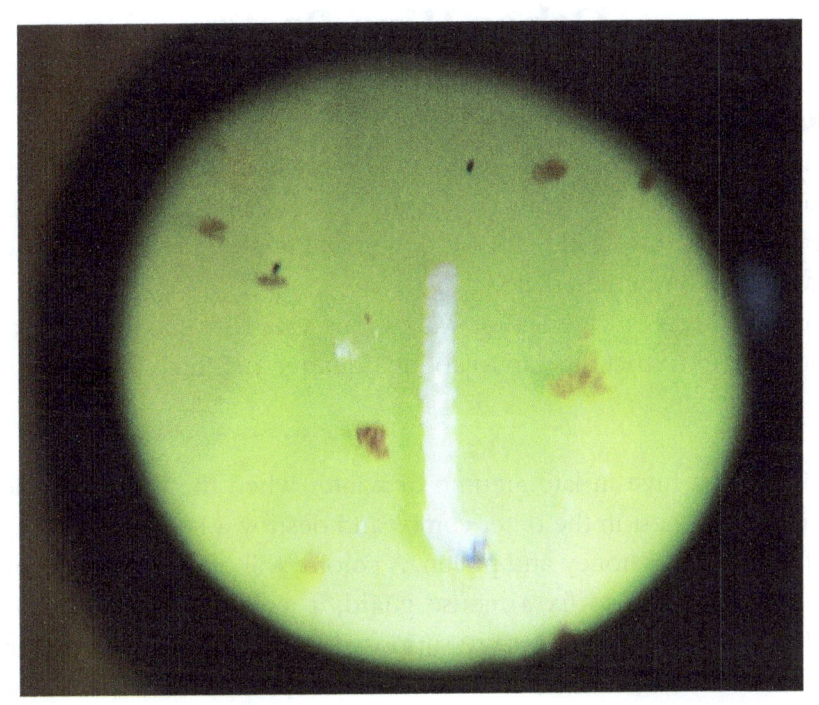

Antenna from varroa infected pupa removed by varroa resistant bees

Acarine

Acarine is a small mite that lives in the bee's trachea, or breathing tubes. It was said to be the cause of the decline of the native British bee in the early 1900's. Bees were imported from Italy and France that were less susceptible to acarine, and have replaced the native strain. There is no approved chemical treatment for acarine.
For details, see:
https://secure.fera.defra.gov.uk/beebase/index.cfm?pageid=192

Generally, colonies that are resistant to varroa are also immune to acarine, since the hygienic strain is intolerant of the presence of mites, wasps and other foreign intruders.

Other diseases that beekeepers worry about, including amoeba, viruses of various types (many brought in by varroa), and threats from foreign introductions such as Small Hive Beetle etc. are described in the above DEFRA web site (BeeBase).

Other Hive Pests

Wasps

From July till the first frosts of Autumn, wasps can be a nuisance and can kill off a hive unless the entrance is small enough to be defended by the guard bees. A wasp trap near the hive will help, but don't bait it with honey! I use apple juice, jam, marmalade or a combination.

To prevent invasion by mice or wasps, put a narrow entrance block in the hive entrance, to restrict the gap to about a quarter inch high by 3 inches wide.

Mice

Mice will enter a hive in late autumn or winter when the bees are quiescent. They will make a nest in the outer combs and destroy a lot of the comb, eating some of the stores of honey and pollen. A colony will often die as a result. One way to prevent this is to fix a mouse guard, a metal sheet with small holes, on the hive entrance. The holes are supposed to be large enough to admit the bees, but small enough to stop a mouse. In my experience a determined mouse will get through somehow. One old beekeeper said that if you could insert an HB pencil into a hive, a mouse will get in. I suppose the same would apply if you checked with a BB or H pencil. I use a queen excluder placed directly below the brood chamber to exclude mice. Make sure that you remove it in the spring!

Woodpeckers

In some areas woodpeckers will attack the hive to get at the brood or the honey. The single walled hives are particularly vulnerable, and the woodpecker pecks a hole in the side wall. The solution is to cover the hive with fine wire mesh, but make sure that it is held about 3 inches (6 cm) from the hive walls, so that the bird can't get a grip to effectively peck at the wall.

Large Mammals

Hives are vulnerable to being knocked over, so make sure that they are fenced in against livestock or animals such as deer and badgers. If you can't find a site sheltered from wind, secure the hive with guy ropes.

Wax Moth

Wax moth is common in empty hives or hives with a lot of old comb and a weak colony. There are two species of wax moth: large and small. The small wax moth eats wax on capped honey. The large wax moth eats mainly old brood comb and pupates in silk cocoons around the edges of brood frames and in crevices in the hive. Wax moth can destroy stored brood comb over winter, but this is not necessarily a bad thing, for old brood comb can harbour diseases such as nosema and European foulbrood. There are chemical remedies for deterring wax moth, but as I said in the introduction to this book, I believe these harm the bees, for both bees and moths are insects. If you want to store comb honey for more than a few months, it is best to put it in the freezer. This also has the benefit of stopping the honey from crystallizing in the comb.

Other Seasonal Operations

The following operations should be done only as the need arises and will depend on the state of your hives, the season and the weather.

Combining Hives

The replacement of a queen is a tricky operation. It is usually done in late summer, when a hive has a queen that is failing due to old age, or the bees are very aggressive. It involves finding the old queen and killing her, then introducing the new queen. It is also risky, in that often the bees will not accept the new queen, so you end up with a queenless hive. In late summer, it is unlikely that the bees will successfully raise their own new queen, so the hive goes into autumn queenless and there are no bees left in it after winter. A far better approach is to merge or combine two hives. This can only be done without major disruption of the colonies if the hives are the same type and have the same dimensions. If you know that one colony is too aggressive, then by all means kill its queen if you can find her before you merge. Otherwise, the more vigorous younger queen will survive the merger and you will end up with a strong hive going into winter, from which you could raise a nucleus the following spring.

If the two hives to be combined are in the same apiary, the weaker hive should be moved next to the stronger hive before they are combined. This may take a few days, depending on how far they are separated, for if a hive is moved more than 3 feet in one day, the foraging bees will return to its old position and not find the new position of the hive. If the hive is moved less than 3 feet, the foraging bees will eventually learn the new position. On the other hand, if the hive is moved more than 3 miles, then the foragers will immediately adapt to their new location. So you can work out the best approach, depending on how far apart your two hives are in the apiary: if more than say 20 feet, it may be best to move the lighter hive to another apiary and leave it there for a week or so, then bring it back to your apiary, sitting beside the other hive.

Combining Warré Hives

To combine the hives, lift off the roof and crown board (or quilt) from the stronger hive, apply smoke from the top and place a single sheet of newspaper to cover the top. Sprinkle a few drops of mint flavoured sugar solution over the middle of the newspaper, then lift the weaker hive off its floor and place it on top of the other hive, with the newspaper in between. The purpose of the newspaper it to prevent the bees from the hive below suddenly encountering those from the hive on top, before they have had a chance to mingle gradually their distinctive hive odours. The minty sugar solution will further mask the difference and so reduce the likelihood of the bees fighting. A few puffs of smoke before they are combined will also help to inhibit any aggression. After a day or so, the bees will have bitten through the newspaper and will be fully integrated in the combined hive.

Combining HTB Hives

Obviously there should be enough space in the HTB for all the brood comb from both hives. If necessary, remove unused or surplus honey combs from both hives. This operation is much trickier than for Warré hives, and will require the use of a smoker.

Move all the remaining combs in the weaker hive to one side of the hive, near to the usual open entrance. Keep the combs in the same order.

Put a bee-proof partition in the middle of the weaker hive.

Carefully lift out the combs from the stronger hive and put them at the other side of the partition, in the same order that they were in their original hive.

Close the hive and open up the entrance for the side into where you transferred the combs. Take away the emptied hive, so that stray bees do not go back into it.

After a couple of days or so, replace the partition with a folded sheet of newspaper, sprinkle about a spoonful of minty sugar solution on it and close up. The bees will gradually bite it away and merge peacefully.

Winter Starvation

Often, after a very cold winter, beekeepers have reported the death of a colony where there was still a good weight of stores left in the hive. They found a cluster of dead bees on the floor and inside empty comb, yet half the remaining combs were full of capped honey. In those sad cases, the cluster of bees had consumed all the honey in the combs which it occupied, working its way upward until reaching the quilt or crown board. Yet because of the cold, the cluster was unable to migrate sideways to the region of remaining honey filled combs, and suffered starvation. To enable the cluster to migrate, there should be enough space under the crown board so that the top of the cluster can move sideways along the top of the frames to settle on those frames where the honey hasn't been consumed.

One way to provide this top space is to put an eke just below the crown board. An eke is a wooden frame of the same outer dimensions as the crown board, and about an inch in height. The time to do this is after taking off the last crop of honey, so that the bees can seal with propolis where it fits between the hive walls and crown board. An eke is usually used to deepen the brood chamber to provide room for deeper brood frames.

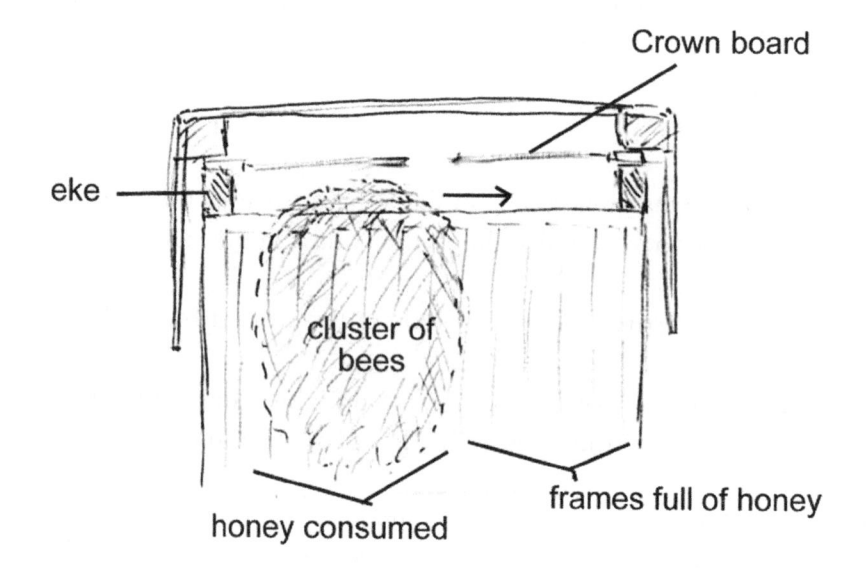

brood frame with eke

If, as in the bitter early spring of 2013 in the UK and Northern Europe, you find that the bees are in danger of consuming all their honey before the first nectar can be gathered, to help them survive, a block of fondant is needed – see chapter Checking Stores. The fondant should be placed directly over the cluster – normally over the feed hole in the crown board, but if the cluster is distant from the feed hole, it may be necessary to carefully place it directly on top of the frames occupied by the cluster. If there is not enough space between the crown board and the top of the frames to place the fondant, then put an eke under the crown board as shown, with a sheet of newspaper to cover it, held in place by the eke. This will allow the bees to feed directly in the fondant, but still under cover of newspaper so that their warmth is contained. See diagram below.

A better food than fondant is the set (crystallised) honey from that same hive, honey that has been saved by the beekeeper as an emergency reserve.

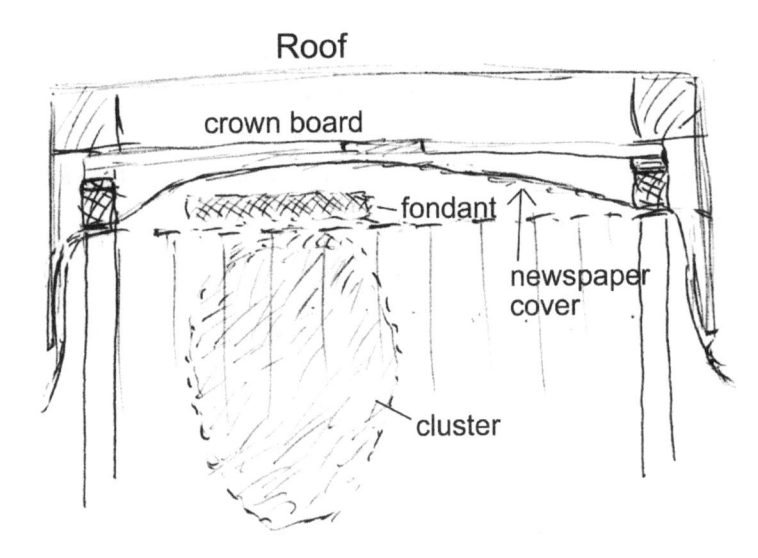

emergency feed of fondant sugar

Post Mortem

If a colony has unfortunately died, a post mortem should be done on it to find the cause of death. It may be simply starvation, or the colony may have succumbed to severe cold, with chilled brood and insufficient young bees hatching to replace the over-wintered bees as they die. On the other hand, it may be due to disease: foulbrood, nosema: see previous chapters. If disease is suspected, the regional bee inspector should be consulted, but in any case you should ask an experienced beekeeper to help in the post mortem.

Except in the case of disease, where the comb and frames and possibly the hive body should be destroyed by burning, any comb from a colony that has died over winter that still has honey should be taken away from the apiary. This is to avoid robbing by bees from other colonies, which could result in fighting between the surviving colonies, and the spreading of disease. If you are sure that the comb isn't diseased, then you could put it on top of a strong surviving colony, where any remaining honey will be taken down. See Annex: Winter Death Post Mortems.

Propagation

Propagation of bees from strong hives is desirable, and can be done as part of the swarm management programme in the summer. The ideal strain of bees to propagate will have the following traits:

1. Docile – easily handled. After lightly smoking and opening the hive to inspect

the brood chamber, the bees do not fly at the beekeeper, intent on stinging. They remain on the comb, quietly working away, rather than frantically running over the comb. Of course, a badly handled colony can be expected to react defensively, and ought to do so.
2. Productive – good foragers and honey producers.
3. Hygienic – removes all debris, rotten comb, wax moth, sick and dying and dead bees.
4. Resistant to attack by pests and diseases, in particular varroa, acarine, wasps.

An efficient programme will aim to increase good quality stock by division, and reduce poor colonies by merging.

For division, see the chapter on *Swarm Control*.

For merging, see the previous chapter.

Propagation of Varroa Resistance within a Local Beekeeping Association

If a beekeeper is fortunate enough to discover a colony that exhibits all the desirable traits listed in the preceding chapter, including hygienic behaviour and vigorous removal of varroa, infected larvae and pupae, then his local association may wish to breed from it. There are many ways of rearing queens that are described in detail in the beekeeping books and journals. They vary in complexity, and their success often depends on the skill of the beekeeper and the circumstances, such as weather, nature and size of the breeding colony etc. The following method is most suitable for propagating the strain for a group of beekeepers who wish to populate a contiguous area of countryside with that strain. It is done by seeding strips of comb with eggs into queenless nuclei that are provided by members of the association, so an almost unlimited number of colonies can be propagated from one hive. Care must be taken to observe hygiene and avoid cross-contamination between hives and nuclei from other apiaries, so don't transfer combs, frames or top bars between nuclei or hives!

Collecting a Swarm

Swarms generally happen from May to July. A swarm will leave the hive on a warm day, usually from late morning till the afternoon. A prime swarm consists of about twenty to thirty thousand bees, which includes the old queen from their parent hive. The bees leave the hive and fly to a nearby tree and settle in a tight cluster on a branch. The cluster is usually the size and shape of a rugby ball, on average 18 inches from top to bottom. There the bees wait, while scout bees will leave the cluster and seek a suitable cavity in which to establish the new colony. This could take any time from less than an hour, to several days, and this is the time to capture the swarm.

To collect the swarm you need a suitable open container, such as a cardboard box about 14 inches square: a grocery box or 6-bottle wine box will do. Some beekeepers use a straw skep. You will also need an old cotton bed sheet if you need to transport the bees some distance from where they were collected. Put on your bee suit, including Wellington boots and rubber gloves. You don't need the smoker. Usually the swarm will have recently left the hive, so the bees will be gorged on honey and reluctant to sting.

The Ideal Swarm

It is remarkable that bees, that are wild creatures and do not depend on the help or intervention of man for survival, will often on swarming from a hive settle on a nearby tree and wait there long enough for the beekeeper to capture them. Of course they don't always do that, sometimes they may have already decided their destination, which may be a suitable cavity in a building, tree or an empty hive, before they leave the hive. But the ideal swarm will settle on a slender branch of a nearby tree, the branch will be no higher than five feet from the ground, and it will be within sight of the hive. All the beekeeper needs to do is to put a suitably sized open cardboard box beneath the cluster (an empty wine box is ideal) and gently jerk the branch upward, when the entire cluster will fall into the box. The foresighted beekeeper will have already laid out a cotton bed sheet on the ground beneath the swarm, before lowering the box onto the sheet, upside down. One side of the box is propped up with a stick or stone to leave a small gap for bees outside to enter, and the well-behaved swarm will start fanning at the entrance to attract their fellows into the box by scent, which is detectable to people, and quite pleasant.

Wait until all the swarm is inside the box, then lift the sheet to enclose the lot, knot it tight and carefully take it to the new hive, still keeping the box inverted. Rather than dumping the swarm into the top of the hive, the polite method is to untie the enclosing bed sheet and lay it over a ramp up to the entrance of the hive, then gently tip the swarm onto the ramp and watch them march up the ramp and into the hive through the entrance. What could possibly go wrong?

Many things could go wrong, causing the swarm to abscond for a number of reasons:
a) the hive entrance is too wide, making them feel vulnerable
b) the swarm is without a queen, or a cast with a flighty virgin queen
c) the swarm has been fed too early after hiving, before the bees have built comb and started to raise brood, so they have enough ingested food and feel confident enough to set out again to find a better home
d) they just don't like the new hive or its location.

The best arrangement is to put shallow frames or bars of old dry comb in the brood chamber, or if the swarm is large in a double brood chamber. Let them settle for several days until you see them bringing in pollen before feeding. A big swarm probably doesn't need feeding at all.

Collecting a well-behaved swarm

Spread out the sheet on flat ground close beneath where the swarm is hanging. Hold the box just under the swarm and gently scoop the bees into the box. If the swarm is hanging awkwardly so that it is difficult to scoop them with the box, use a flat piece of card to sweep them into the box.

As soon as the swarm is disturbed, many of the bees will fly around. Don't worry, so long as the majority are in the box.

Put the box on the ground, upside down, in the middle of the sheet. Tilt the box slightly to leave a gap of about an inch between it and the ground sheet, propping it up about an inch with a stick or stone, to allow the bees to fly in and out of the box.

You will notice that any bees left on the branch will gradually fly off and enter the box. If they don't, they will return to the branch. If the branch is thin enough to be cut off with secateurs or a lopper, then it may be easier to remove it and take it down to the ground and put it and the swarm inside the box before inverting the box. After an hour or so, the bees will be in the box, clustered and hanging inside. It may be best to wait till the evening to give all the bees time to settle.

When you are happy that all the bees are inside the box (apart from a few stragglers), lift the corners of the sheet, gather and tie the top together to fully enclose the box and the bees. You can now safely move the bees to the new hive, but make sure the box is steady in the car and upside down with the cluster quietly hanging inside. Take the bees to the new hive.

Hiving the Swarm

There are several ways that swarms can be introduced into the hive, depending on the type of hive, the nature and size of the swarm, and the weather.

Method 1 - Warré
With top bars or frames of comb or foundation in the hive, put the box down in front of the entrance, then unknot the sheet and lay it out up to the hive entrance. Lift the box sharply and the clustered bees will fall onto the sheet and start to walk up to the hive entrance and go inside. This is the polite way of introducing them into the hive rather than just dumping them in, but it is unsuitable for an HTB hive.

Method 2 - Warré
If the swarm is not large, set up a brood box with top bars or frames of comb or foundation, or just empty frames if you have no spare comb or foundation ready. Put the crown board on top, then lift the swarm box sharply above the hive so that the bulk of the cluster falls on top. Shake off any bees that are still clinging inside the box. The cluster will enter the hive through the feed hole – see photograph.

Swarm entering hive from top

This swarm was collected in a straw skep, which can be seen in front of the hive. You can see the bees aligned towards the feed holes on the crown board. Some have their tails in the air, fanning their wings, wafting the homing odour to the rest who may be flying around, telling them to follow. You should be able to smell that odour yourself. Most of the bees are already inside the hive, and when all bar a few stragglers are in, put the roof on top.

Method 3 - Warré
With top bars or frames of comb or foundation in the hive, open the top of the hive and take off the crown board. Dump the bees from the box into the top of the hive, then gently rest the crown board on top. There will be bees underneath, so the crown board will be resting on the cluster, but as the cluster goes down into the hive the crown board will settle to rest on top of the hive.

Method 4 - HTB
Depending on the size of the swarm, put a row of 12 to 25 top bars on the hive, close up to the side you chose as the entrance. Remove the other top bars and partition panel and bung up all bar one entrance on the other side. Hold the swarm box upside down above the hive where there are no bars, and sharply lift it so that the bulk of the swarm falls into the hive. It should move into the hive, towards the dark under the top bars. Shake any remaining bees into the hive and gently brush any bees that are walking over the top bars into the hive. Close up the hive with the remaining top bars and place the partition panel to give the colony enough space: usually about half the hive length, depending on the size of the swarm. See diagram.

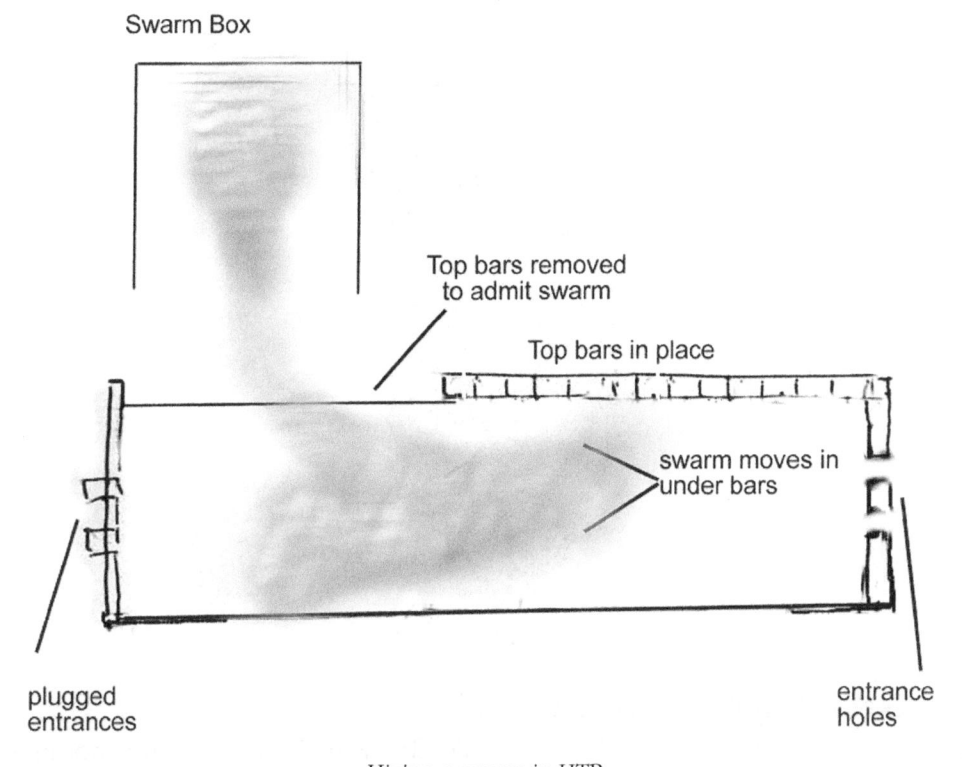

Hiving a swarm in HTB

Absconding
To reduce the chances of a captured swarm leaving its new hive, the bees must feel secure and comfortable. There must be enough room in the hive to prevent overcrowding, and the entrance must be restricted so that they feel that they can defend it. It also helps if there is some old comb there. I have collected many a swarm merely by leaving an empty hive with some old comb in it, and there is

a good chance that a swarm will find it and enter by itself – vacant possession! These empty hives are sometimes called "Bait Hives". It is important also not to feed a swarm until you know that it has settled into the new hive, since after having fed, the swarm may have enough confidence to set off again to find a better home. You can tell that it has settled if they start to bring in pollen.

Small swarm hanging from a tree

Transferring Comb to a Frame

If you have a colony that has built "wild comb", which is comb that is not in a frame and so cannot be manipulated when you inspect the bees, then you may need to transfer it. This could happen if a swarm has entered a hive without a full complement of top bars or framed combs or foundation, or you have left the swarm in its cardboard box as in case c) above. If you have a Warré or HTB you will need to make up frames that will fit into your hive, and tie the wild comb into those frames. It is not possible to securely fix comb to a top bar.

To put the combs in a frame, prepare an empty frame by tying stout cotton threads to the top bar and bottom bar as shown in figure.

Frame for wild comb

Top Bar

cotton thread

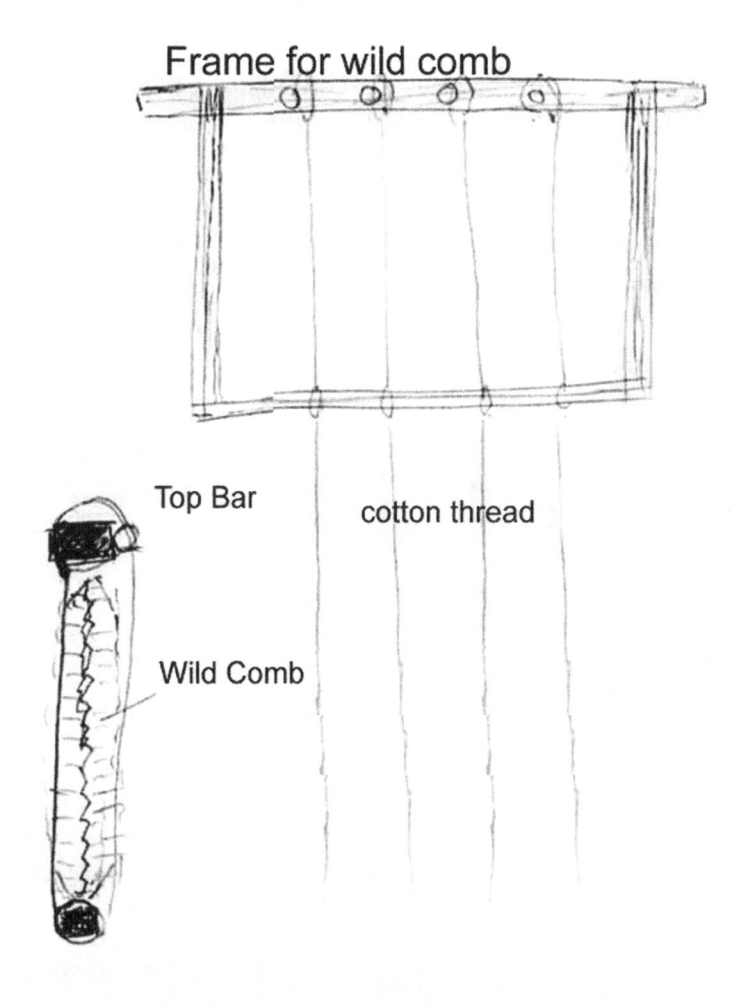

Wild Comb

Put the hive into which you are going to transfer the comb next to the box or hive with the wild comb. The destination hive should contain enough empty frames with cotton thread to receive the wild comb, plus top bars or frames of comb or foundation to make a full set for the brood chamber. Lay a frame with the cotton thread horizontally on the top bars of brood chamber, letting the hanging ends of the threads drop over the outside of the hive.

Cut a piece of wild comb out from where it is fixed in the cardboard swarm box or source hive. Use a very sharp knife, to avoid disturbing the bees. Try not to cut into brood cells, and use your smoker to clear the bees from your cutting edge. Gently place the comb inside the frame, to rest horizontally on the tight threads between the top bar and bottom bar. The top of the wild comb should be close to the top bar.

Lift the hanging thread ends over the comb and tie them tight to the top bar of the frame, to firmly hold the wild comb inside the frame. You should be able to lift the frame horizontally without the comb falling out. Put the frame into the brood chamber, and do the same with all the wild comb. You only need to bother with wild comb that has brood or substantial amounts of honeycomb.

Put the crown board then the roof over the brood chamber. If there are some small wild combs with honey still remaining in the swarm box, put an empty super on top of the hive and put those combs inside. The bees will take the honey down into the hive and the empty comb can be taken out later and stored for wax extraction.

Brood and honey comb tied into frame

After a day or so the bees will have fixed the comb in the frame and bitten away the cotton thread.

Colonies in Buildings and Trees

Sometimes the beekeeper will be asked to remove a colony from a building. Usually it will be in a chimney, roof or cavity wall.

It is almost impossible to transfer the colony to a hive by cutting away the comb from the fabric of the building and taking it away in a box, for most of the bees will fly from the comb and return to same place in the building, even if all the comb is removed. You will end up with a sticky mess of brood and honey comb in the box, with dead or dying bees. Those that escape will re-colonise the building and either restore their nest or die off over winter.

There are ways of smoking out the bees, or sucking them out by vacuum, or drumming them up a chimney into a skep. Some books tell you to put a one-way bee escape such as a cloth funnel over the opening where the bees enter and leave the building, with a empty hive on a platform next to it, in the hope that the bees will occupy the hive. However you will need to provide a new queen for the empty hive, for the queen in the building will not venture through the trap into the new hive. Also, it is likely that the bees will find an alternative entrance to their old cavity. I advise you to decline to remove an established colony from a building, and leave it as a good source of possibly varroa resistant swarms.

If the colony is in a tree, the same argument will apply: leave well alone. If the tree has been felled, then it may be possible to hive it by sawing the trunk above and below the colony, fixing it upright on the ground. Ensure that there is a clear passage for the bees to fly in and out of the top of the sawn off tree trunk, either by sawing off the top bit of the trunk just above the hollow where the bees live, or by chiselling or drilling a hole through the top. Then put a crown board on top, and then put a brood box with frames of comb or foundation on top of the crown board. Make sure the whole arrangement is secure and stable. Block off any side to the trunk and with any luck over a few seasons the colony will migrate up to the empty hive. Failing that, they may swarm or in a good season even put honey in the hive!

Bee Friendly Environment

Post-War agricultural policies have devastated our countryside wildlife. Hedges have been grubbed out in order to extend arable acreage, orchards cut down and the use of insecticides, herbicides and fertilisers renders both arable and pastoral land into a green desert, hostile to insects and the birds and small mammals that feed on them. Indeed, the environment of cities and large towns is more beneficial to bees, and beekeepers in London and Birmingham have harvested more honey than those in the countryside. Too many home gardeners and town councils are obsessed with neatly manicured lawns, closely mown fields and weed free verges. Pollinating insects don't have a chance, and many butterflies and bumblebees are becoming extinct.

Fortunately there is a movement driven by the celebrated gardener Sarah Raven, which is restoring our native meadows and hedgerows. She has persuaded some enlightened farmers to allow boundary strips of uncultivated ground to become meadows. A beneficial side effect is that insect and bird predators of crop pests are allowed to thrive, so reducing the farmers' reliance on insecticides. Some gardeners are now allowing their gardens to grow wild flowers, and so enjoy their natural beauty and the butterflies that visit them. They also save petrol and the accompanying fumes, noise and wasted effort of mowing and strimming.

So what are the best plants for honeybees? Starting from early spring, the following are some of the honeybees' favourites:

Snowdrop, witch hazel, willow, crocus, cherry (not ornamental), all soft fruit (raspberry, gooseberry, blackcurrant, strawberry), dandelion, plum, pear, apple, hawthorn, cotoneaster (an insignificant flower, but the bees go mad on it), white clover (the weather must be warm), bramble, which is the main source of honey in the countryside, willowherb (fireweed). Himalayan balsam is considered to be a pernicious weed that clogs rivers, but it is to be welcomed by beekeepers as a marvellous source of very fine pale honey. All sorts of flowering shrubs, generally with small flowers, give off significant amounts of nectar. Then the large trees: horse chestnut, lime, sweet chestnut, honeydew secreted by aphids: a lovely dark viscous honey is produced from it. Finally, the autumn flowers – asters, heather, goldenrod, and almost into winter, ivy.

spare the mower! - wild flowers on my uncut orchard

The Joys of Beekeeping

In this short book I have given a detailed account of the essential operations that a beekeeper performs throughout the year. I have outlined the nature and lifecycle of the honeybee, sufficient to give a basic understanding of its behaviour in order to efficiently manage your hives. If you want to read further about the natural history and detailed biology of the honeybee, or on specialised practices such a queen rearing, there are many fine publications available.

There are few moments in life that match the joy of standing near a healthy hive on a warm day, when the bees are flying and bringing in their loads of sweet nectar and colourful pollen. To hear the humming of the hive and smell the intoxicating aroma of the evaporating nectar on a warm summer evening gives a feeling of peace and tranquillity that is rarely experienced in our mundane and hectic modern world: a true communion with nature.

Further Reading

This book describes my approach to beekeeping where I have attempted to reduce to a minimum the beekeeper's intervention in the colony. It also aims to provide guidance and encouragement to new beekeepers and experienced beekeepers who want to cease chemical treatment of their hives. However, it is not intended to provide a comprehensive encyclopaedia on all aspects of apiculture, which already has an extensive body of literature. Here are a few books that cover the biology of the honeybee, and advanced practices such as Queen Rearing, Swarm Prevention, Hive Design etc.

1. **The New Complete Guide to Beekeeping** - Roger A. Morse (1994)
   ISBN 978-0881503159
   I bought the earlier edition of this book when I started beekeeping in 1979, before the onset of varroa. I found it very useful, though it was written for beekeeping in North America. Obviously, in the UK we do not suffer from bears and skunks, nor do we need to over-winter hives in jackets of straw covered with tarpaper. However, bearing in mind the differences in climate, the insight into beekeeping in America was interesting and instructive.

2. **The BBKA Guide to Beekeeping** – Ivor Davis and Roger Cullum-Kenyon (2012)
   ISBN 978-1-4081-5458-8
   A comprehensive guide, giving extensive coverage on the biology of the bee, bee diseases and swarm management.

3. **Queen Breeding and Genetics – How to get better bees** – Eigil Holm
   ISBN 978-1-904846-62-8
   This book covers the rearing and mating of queens, as well as the evolution, genetics, and races of bees. A useful reference for hobbyist beekeepers as well as specialist queen breeders.

4. **Beekeeping for All** – Abbé Émile Warré (2010)
   Translated from: 'L'Apiculture Pour Tous' (12th ed., 1948) by Patricia and David Heaf
   ISBN: 978-1-904846-52-9
   As well as describing the construction of the Warré top bar hive, the Abbé has much to say about the breeding of bees to improve honey yields and the undesirability of medication to treat diseases including foulbrood. Of course

he was writing long before the scourge of varroa and modern agrichemicals, but his words of wisdom, based on his experiences of beekeeping throughout a long life, are very relevant today.

5. **Research on Varroa Resistant Bees in Russia and USA**
   http://www.ars.usda.gov/Services/docs.htm?docid=2744&page=15&pf=1&cg_id=0
   The end of this article, published in the United States Department of Agriculture web site, gives a detailed description of the reproductive timescale of the varroa mite, alongside the development of the worker bee. It describes how bees from Eastern Russia, that demonstrated inherent resistance to varroa, were imported into the USA and used in breeding trials. The article refers to research papers on the subject, including the observations of Ibrahim and Spivak recorded in the American Bee Journal 2003, 144:406, that bees with the inherited trait of mite suppression selectively removed pupae from the cells that had reproductive mites.

6. **A Simple Method of Raising Queen Cells** – Ben Harden N.D.B.
   - a booklet in the series "Beekeeping in a Nutshell", Number 59
   Northern Bee Books (same publishers of the paperback of this book, see frontispiece.
   Email – www.northernbeebooks.co.uk

7. **The determination of the sexes of honebees.**
   http://www.nature.com/scitable/topicpage/sex-determination-in-honeybees-2591764

ANNEX

1. Colony Losses since stopping Chemical Treatment

The first table below show my experience with colony losses since I stopped treating my hives with chemicals in 2000. The second table is a summary of recent experience of our local group of Natural Beekeepers in the Frome and Bruton area of East Somerset.

Year	Hives after Winter	Total Honey Crop (pounds)	Hives before Next Winter	Loss	Gain
2000	0	90	4 (1 bought, 1 nucleus, 2swarm)		4
2001	4	169	5 (2 swarms, 2 merged)	0	1
2002	3	60	4 (1 swarm entered*)	2	1
2003	3 (mice)	128	5 (1 nucleus, 1 swarm entered)	1	2
2004	4	45	5 (1 swarm entered)	1	1
2005	1 (2 starved, 1 queenless)	27	4 (3 swarms entered)	4	3
2006	3	19	3	1	0
2007	2	16 ivy	3 (1 swarm entered)	1	1
2008	3	35	3	0	0
2009	2 (1 knocked over)	50 +38 ivy	3 (1 swarm entered)	1	1
2010	3	35	1 (1 paralysis, 1 wasps)	2	
2011	1 (v. cold isolated cluster)	0 (cold wet summer)	2 (1 small cast caught)	0	1
2012	2	50 (cold v. wet summer)	3 (1 swarm entered, merged with 1 queenless swarm)	0	1
2013	2	30 (bitter spring: chilled brood)	5 (+1 split hive + 2 nuclei raised from the same colony)	1	3

* "swarm entered" means that a swarm, usually from a feral colony, entered my empty hive.

Colony Gains/Losses by Natural Beekeepers in East Somerset (Frome/Bruton)

Colonies before winter 2012	Colonies after winter 2012/13	Main cause of winter losses	Gains in Summer 2013	Colonies October 2013	Colonies after winter 2013/14
21	13	Bitterly cold March resulting in starvation and/or chilled brood	22 from swarms, 3 from splits.	25	24

The conclusions from these tables are:
a) Very cold wet summers from 2006/8 and 2010/12 account for my poor honey crops.
b) Inexplicable colony losses that can be attributed to varroa (i.e. no bees dead or alive in the hive on the first inspection after winter) were at a peak in 2004 to 2005. Since then, increase has been mainly from feral swarms entering my empty hives, and their survival chances are increasing.

In England and Wales, the figures published by the Food and Environment Agency for colony losses from 1999 to 2008 show a steady increase from 5% to 12%.
See https://secure.fera.defra.gov.uk/beebase/downloadNews.cfm?id=60
The BBKA press release of June 2012 gives the losses from 2007 – 2012:

2007/8	2008/9	2009/10	2010/11	2011/12	2012/13
30.5%	18.7%	17.7%	13.6%	16.2%	33.8%

http://www.bbka.org.uk/files/library/bbka_winter_survival_survey_release_final_14_june_1339663845.pdf

Explanations given for the 2011/12 losses were:
a) Queen related problems such as drone laying queens
b) Clusters unable to reach food reserves in the hive
c) Poor weather affecting queen mating
d) Increased wasp activity possibly due to mild autumn

I think the hives that succumbed to wasp attack were dosed with thymol preparations such as Apiguard™ and Apistan™. The scent of thymol is strong and disrupts the natural scents of the hive and colony pheromones, so confusing the bees who cannot distinguish friend from foe. Anecdotal data from beekeepers in the Frome area of Somerset indicates very high losses (around 50%) in the winter of 2011-12, by beekeepers who treated their hives with chemicals.

The explanation for the increased 2012/13 losses was the wet and cold summer of 2012: poor foraging and virgin queens were not properly mated. The survey went out in February 2013, and I am sure the losses were even greater, about 50%. In March the weather became even colder and the weaker hives were unable to cover the brood, so there were no young bees to replace the overwintered bees.

In the USA in 2011, the winter losses were 30%.

See http://www.ibra.org.uk/articles/US-honey-bee-winter-colony-losses-2010-11

2. Winter Death Post Mortems

The following are some typical findings from colonies that have died over winter:

1. Colony Starvation:

Symptoms: Thousands of dead bees on the comb, their heads stuck in cells emptied of honey.

Cause: Not enough honey left in the hive!

Remedy: There should be at least 27 pounds (12 kg) of honey in the hive for winter. Weigh the hive before October (or November if there is a strong inflow of ivy nectar) and if light, feed with sugar solution (see Preparing for Winter).

2. Cluster Isolated from Stores:

Symptoms: most of the frames in the hive have capped honey, but thousands of dead bees on empty comb or on the floor, isolated from the combs full of honey. There may be still a small cluster of live bees on comb with honey, but separated from the rest. They may survive if the season is kind.

Cause: Extreme cold weather, preventing bees from migrating as a cluster to combs that still have honey.

Remedy: On a cold calm day in late winter or early spring, check whether the cluster is seen just below the feed hole, then place a block of fondant over it. If the cluster is distant from the feed hole, lift the crown board and place the fondant over the top of the cluster, or put thin slices of fondant in the gaps between the frames which the cluster occupies. See Winter Starvation.

3. Mouse damage:

Symptoms: Mouse nest inside the brood chamber.

Cause: A mouse entered the hive in late autumn when the bees were drowsy and bit holes in the brood frames at one side of the hive, then made a nest of dried leaves and grass inside those damaged frames. Sometimes a strong colony will survive.

Remedy: Use a narrow entrance block and make sure there are no other holes in the hive walls. The slot in the entrance should be less than 0.8 cm or 5/16 inch.

4. Failed Queen

Symptoms: A few dead bees, plenty of stores, mouldy comb.

Cause: The queen was old or an unmated virgin, or was not properly mated due to poor weather or lack of drones at the time of the mating flights.

Remedy: Examine hive in late summer. If little or no pollen is being brought in, this is a sign that the Queen is not laying. Check the brood frames for capped and uncapped brood, and to see if there are any eggs present. If not, remove the Queen (if you can find her) and replace with a new mated queen. This is a risky procedure in Autumn, so it will be safer to merge the hive with one that is bringing in pollen, provided you are sure that the barren hive is not diseased (see Combining Hives).

5. Varroa

Symptoms: A few dead bees, hive still full of honey, piles of dead varroa on the floor.

Cause: The colony succumbed to varroa.

Remedy: See chapter on Varroa.

3. Herbal Remedy for Nosema

This is a recipe sent to me by Natural Beekeeper Adam Brocklehurst, known as "Brock". I tried it on one of my hives that showed signs of chronic nosema in the early summer, and they recovered to produce a good crop of honey in the dreadful English Summer of 2012.

Hi all, firstly thank you very much to Rowena for her hospitality, what a great place she has.

Also thanks to Joe for sharing his knowledge and adventures with us.

I have found some information on feeding bees, which I hope will be of help.

SYRUP OF SAGE HONEY

Approx four dessert spoons of honey [your own or from a very reliable source, bearing in mind disease etc], more or less depending on your preference.
One pint of water,
Half a pint of "mother" cider vinegar,[1]
Half a cup of finely chopped sage,
Apple cores or rosehips if available [they help to prevent scouring]

Make a standard brew of the sage and water;
    put herbs/apple cores/rosehips [finely shredded with scissors] and cold water

in to a saucepan,

cover tightly with a well fitting lid to prevent loss of vital oils, and heat over a slow fire to near boiling [do not boil].

Hold it there for one to two minutes and then remove from heat and leave to stand, keeping covered at all times.

When it is tepid add the honey and vinegar, cover and let stand for at least three hours, better for six hours or overnight.

When cool pour in to the hive feeding trough.

If you have to use brown sugar instead of honey then add a pinch of salt as this helps prevent scour.

The author has much disregard for white sugar as it is a cause of general health decline in bees [and people].2

It is also recommended that a rock from the sea is placed in to the bees water bowl .

I have to say I have no practical experience to compare with this but to me this all makes a great deal of sense.

The beekeeping experience comes from a Spanish beekeeper with a reputation for excellent honey, the herbal experience is from my favourite and most trusted herbal veterinarian, Juliette De Bairacli Levy.

> *Happy beeing inspired,*
> *Brock*

1. I used vinegar made from my own cider, according to my book "Make Cider without Fuss or Chemicals", also available on Kindle.
2. I would not use brown sugar to feed bees, since it contains some substances that are bad for the bee's gut, according to Dr Julian M Cooper, Head of Food Science, British Sugar plc, writing in the BBKA News February 2010. White sugar is OK, but honey from your own hive is better. You may have taken off ivy honey from previous years, to make room in a hive that was clogged with combs of hard set ivy honey. Save that for this sort of use, since the taste of ivy honey is too strong for many people.

Tales of Swarms

- a few anecdotes from my early days in beekeeping, with lessons learnt!

How I started beekeeping

Insects fascinated me since childhood: butterflies, ants and bees. I remember asking my grandmother about the different types of bees that visited the flowers in her garden, and wondering what it would be like to keep a hive. But it was not till my mid thirties that I developed a serious interest when one Saturday morning a neighbour came along the gravel drive past our garden, asking if I had seen a swarm. He was John Purkiss, a retired Royal Navy officer, then a member of the Baltic Exchange in London. He said that he was looking after several hives in his orchard that were left by a friend who had emigrated to India. I said that I had not seen a swarm, but was interested in bees. He proposed that I partner him in beekeeping and if I took it up I could put my own hives in his orchard apiary. John himself was new to beekeeping, and had joined the local beekeeping association in Wokingham. It had its own apiary, which was looked after by Mr. Sprague, a very experienced beekeeper. They held apiary meetings during the summer, and new beekeepers learned from his advice and friendly encouragement. So I joined the association and bought a hive of bees from a man who was leaving the area to live in Devon.

We lived in the village of Eversley in North East Hampshire, at that time a mixed environment of woods, grazing, forestry, heath, country estates and gardens. Though we didn't find John's swarm, there was never a shortage of swarms. Many of them emanated from the roofs of old houses in Eversley such as Warbrook and Saint Neot's preparatory school. So my early beekeeping years involved a lot of swarm collecting – climbing ladders, crawling along the roofs of tall buildings, trying to persuade bees to leave cavity walls and so on. Of course, there were many false alarms to investigate: wasp nests and bumble bees, but that was part of the job, to reassure members of the public.

I will tell you about my most memorable experiences in swarm collection over the years, starting with the "ideal" swarm

The Ideal Swarm

It is remarkable that bees, who are wild creatures that do not depend on the help or intervention of man for survival, will often on leaving the hive settle on a nearby tree and wait there long enough for the beekeeper to capture them.

Of course they don't always do that, sometimes they may have already chosen their final destination before they leave the hive, which may be a suitable cavity in a building, tree or an empty hive. Often I've visited my hives and found a swarm occupying one of my empty hives, though none of my hives had swarmed. They usually were very productive colonies too. But here I am talking about swarms for collection rather than taking up vacant possession by their own initiative.

The ideal swarm will choose a slender branch of a nearby tree, the branch will be no higher than five feet from the ground, and it will be within sight of the hive whence it came. All the beekeeper needs to do is to put a suitably sized open cardboard box beneath the hanging swarm (an empty wine box is ideal) and gently jerk the branch upward, when the entire cluster will fall into the box. The foresighted beekeeper will have already laid out a cotton bed sheet on the ground beneath the swarm, before lowering the box onto the sheet, upside down. One side of the box is propped up with a stick or stone to leave a small gap for bees outside to enter, and the well-behaved swarm will start fanning at the entrance to attract their fellows into the box by scent, which is detectable to people, and quite pleasant.

the ideal swarm

Wait until all the bees are inside the box, then lift the sheet to enclose the lot, knot it tight and carefully take it to the new hive, still keeping the box inverted. Rather than unceremoniously dumping the swarm into the top of the hive, the polite method is to untie the enclosing bed sheet and lay it over a ramp up to the entrance of the hive, then gently tip the swarm onto the ramp and watch them march up the ramp and into the hive through the entrance. What could possibly go wrong?

The Indian Ladder Trick

One fine Saturday I spotted a swarm on the end of a branch of a tree near our apiary. This swarm would have been ideally placed if it were five feet from the ground, but the branch where it had clustered was nearly twenty feet high, so I needed a ladder. I managed to set up the ladder, leaning it against the branch on the trunk side of the swarm. The branch was thin enough to lop off with secateurs, and I wasn't going to make the classic mistake of cutting the branch between the trunk and the ladder! Nevertheless, it was quite precarious, for the top of the ladder at its full extent was only three inches above where it leaned against the slender branch.

Up I climbed, in full beekeeping outfit including Wellington boots, with a cardboard box in one hand and secateurs in the other. I cut off the branch close to the swarm, holding the box beneath the swarm, and the whole cluster of bees fell nicely into the box. It was quite a heavy swarm and I was pleased, until I noticed with alarm that the branch, now relieved of the weight of the swarm, was slowly lifting against the ladder and within a couple of seconds the ladder was resting on thin air. The ladder, with nothing to lean against, started to topple forward, accelerating from the vertical. I soon realised my situation: I'd heard of the Indian Rope Trick, where a fakir throws a rope into the air and then climbs up it. I had to do the trick in reverse and so I climbed down the ladder as rapidly as I could, still clutching the swarm box full of bees. But gravity beat me – I jumped off the ladder before it hit the ground, fell down and was deposited with the box and its contents into the ditch below, which was full of nettles. The bees were all right – they had wings! They indignantly flew up in a cloud and settled on the remaining bit of the branch whence they came. I was flustered and furious with myself and walked home to decide my next course of action. On my way back I saw a neighbour, who had witnessed the whole operation. When I next went into my local, the White Hart, I was greeted with amusement, for the tale had spread.

To finish the story, I returned to the tree with a saw. No more Mr Nice Guy, I leant the ladder against the tree trunk and sawed off the entire branch after tying a rope to it and looping it pulley fashion over a higher branch then fixing the end of the rope to the stem of a bush at ground level. This time I lowered the branch gently to the ground and so was able to successfully capture the swarm. I'd learnt one lesson: a prime swarm carries weight!

The Hostile Swarm

Though swarms when flying are an impressive sight, and intimidating for non-beekeepers, the general beekeeping experience of swarms is that they are not hostile. Beekeeping literature gives the reason for their lack of aggressiveness in that they gorge themselves on honey before they leave the hive, and this inhibits deployment of the sting. However there are always exceptions, and one evening I came upon such a swarm.

I received a phone call in late July from my friend Arthur after I came home from work. He lived in a leafy district of Fleet in Hampshire, 7 miles away from my home. He told me that there was a swarm hanging on a branch of an apple tree in his neighbour's garden. So I set off in my car after checking and loading my swarm catching kit: cardboard box, cotton bed sheet, bee suit, gloves and secateurs.

The swarm was a good size prime swarm, quietly settled on the branch of a mature apple tree. The neighbour was on holiday, and Arthur wouldn't let me cut off the branch to lower it into the box, so I decided to shake the bees off it. I had to climb up the tree to get at the branch, which was not difficult. Then I shook it, and let loose pandemonium. The bees took off in an angry cloud and soon found my weak spot: my ankles. I had forgotten to take my Wellington boots, so had tucked the bottom of the legs of my overalls into my socks. I was stung about a dozen times through the socks on each ankle and it was too late to borrow Arthur's boots. I just upended the box on the ground under the apple tree and left the scene promptly. The swarm clustered back on the branch whence they were so rudely shaken. It was now dusk and I didn't want to repeat the fiasco, so I left. I promised to come back the next morning, which was a Saturday, hoping that the swarm would fly away in the mean time and save me further humiliation.

On the next morning, a Saturday, Arthur phoned, saying that the swarm had migrated quietly into the box. I made sure that I had full protection on my second visit. With trepidation I gingerly lifted the box containing the swarm over the sheet and tied the sheet round it without any trouble. The swarm was surprisingly heavy, certainly not what I would call a "dry swarm", where the bees have consumed all their ingested honey. It went into one of my old hives without any fuss and immediately set to work, clearing out old dry comb and bringing in pollen and propolis. I could hear the busy rustling as the bees cleaned out the old comb and deposited the debris in front of the hive and set up home. I inspected the hive a fortnight later, feeling apprehensive about their hostility, but they were very docile and productive – perhaps grateful for a new home?

The lesson I learnt from this is to be careful with unknown bees and always wear full protection, even with swarms.

Fishing for a Swarm

There is a limit to how far I am willing to risk my neck in climbing ladders or trees, and this limit is getting lower as I get older. My reactions get slower and my nerve gets weaker with age and experience – my wife says I'm becoming more sensible. But the swarm I was called to would have challenged an intrepid woodsman. It was hanging from the lower branch of a Scots Pine in the garden of a bungalow in our neighbourhood. The pine was part of the larger plantation of oak and pine in Eversley Lower Common, so all the trees were tall in that area. The branch of interest was about fifty feet above the ground, way above the length of my ladder, or if a long enough ladder were available, way above the height that I was prepared to climb.

The tree stood in the garden of friends, Callum and Margaret, who had two children and were worried that they might be stung. Callum, a persuasive Irishman and an angler, suggested the following course of action: shoot a line over the branch, tie the chain of a chainsaw to each end to form a loop, pull it up and over the branch and then back and forth to saw it off. It should then fall down with the swarm. He had all the equipment for it: a nylon fishing line, a lead sinker, a catapult that he used for propelling ground bait into the swim, a long length of strong cord and a spare chain for his chainsaw. After explaining his ingenious plan he went back into the house with his family to watch me execute it through the safety of their lounge window.

I donned my full beekeeping kit and put an empty hive on the ground beneath the tree. Callum's plan worked brilliantly, up to a point. I fired the lead sinker attached to the nylon line from the catapult, aiming to loop it over the branch and descend to the ground. I succeeded on the second attempt, and attached the cord to the end of the nylon line and reeled it up over the branch and down to the ground on the other side. Then I tied the saw chain to each end of the cord, to form a loop, and pulled it up to the branch. By pulling the cord back and forth I managed to saw through the branch.

Up to that point the bees were quietly hanging on the end of the branch, feeling only the force of gravity and the gentle breezes wafting through the pines. As the branch descended, gravitational force suddenly ceased and the breeze was replaced by the rush of air approaching terminal velocity. Those bees that still managed to cling together were rudely jerked off when the branch hit the ground, and so the whole swarm became airborne. It promptly rose up and settled on a higher branch of the same tree. I gave up at that point. Reassuring Callum and Margaret that the bees were much less of a threat to their children now they were on a higher branch, I went home, leaving my empty hive below the tree in case the swarm should be attracted to it, an unlikely eventuality.

So what lesson did I learn from this? The plan was incomplete, said Callum helpfully. We should have pulled up a second cord or rope with a slip knot and secured it to the trunk side of the branch before cutting it. Then we could have lowered the branch gently to the ground. What a good idea! Today that is standard tree surgeon's practice, but then no one bothered about such refinements, except the bees. Since then I've never had the need to try it out.

What became of the swarm? It saw sense after a cold night in the pines and decided to seek better accommodation. It took off the next day across St Neot's road and settled on a slim branch in an oak tree, which I was able to climb. And so the swarm was caught at last!

The Pink Queen

In my early days of beekeeping I used to mark the Queen. Now I don't bother, I can tell whether a hive is queenright if there are eggs and brood. Nor do I clip her wings – I think it's too risky and some would think it cruel and possibly shorten her life. In one nucleus I raised a nice queen successfully and marked her with the only non-toxic paint that I had at the time – some pink nail varnish that my wife no longer used. She looked very pretty (the Queen, as well as my wife) and laid a good brood pattern (the Queen). I hived the nucleus in a Commercial brood box and they built up nicely for over wintering. I was hoping for a good strong colony the following season.

It was one Saturday in the following June that my fellow beekeeper John Purkiss called, saying that one of his empty hives was taken over by a swarm. Would I help him check it out? John's approach to pacifying his bees was to smoke his pipe while opening up the hive, mainly to calm himself rather than the bees. The pipe stem fitted through a hole in his veil, which was as a consequence hardly bee-proof. So he usually recruited me to help him, mainly on the insistence of his wife Belinda.

We looked inside his hive, a WBC. The swarm had settled in nicely, with new wax and brood, and we even managed to spot the queen. I recognised her immediately, pointing her out to John. She was quite obvious from the dab of pink nail varnish on the back of her thorax, where I had marked her the year before. I refused his offer to return the swarm, saying that it had chosen his hive as its new home and so belonged to him.

My hives were single walled: Commercial and National. My daughter always wanted me to get a WBC hive since she said they were much prettier, with their chalet style architecture. There are fewer WBC hives about these days, beekeepers preferring the single-walled hives as being easier to open up. But there is much to be said in favour of the WBC, particularly after the cold winter in Britain of 2012 – 13, and the bitter spring that killed off so many colonies. The outside wall of the WBC provides an extra layer of protection against the biting wind. My son has a WBC hive on his land a thousand feet above sea level in Mid Wales. It over wintered on a double brood chamber and came through very strongly through the winter of 2012-13, when many of the colonies in Montgomeryshire were wiped out.

Any lesson learnt by this swarm? Should I have clipped the Queen's wing when I marked her? I don't think so, there is a risk of damaging her and I think it's unnatural. I don't even bother to seek and mark queens now, since I can tell if the hive has a good queen from the brood pattern.

A Swarm Worth Collecting

In July 2011 I was called by the Environmental Officer who reported a small swarm in Bruton. He was familiar with bees and said that it was a very small swarm, probably a mating cast, and probably not worth collecting, but since he had my number he decide to phone me in case I were interested. Since I lived only a couple of miles away I decided to have a look, and put my kit in the car. The only collecting box I had was a square 20 litre bagged cider container, without its bag.

I was shown the swarm, clinging against a stone wall beside the junction of Plox and Cole Road. I scooped the swarm into the box and put it upside down against the wall. At first the bees entered the box, but after a couple of minutes we noticed that they began to disperse. They swirled over the road and settled in the hedge on the other side - they didn't like the box. It may have been the residual smell of cider in the box, so it took off. I left them there and went home to collect a pair of secateurs and a small straw skep that my son had given me. The bees liked the skep, and I hived them later in a nucleus box, for there were barely enough bees to fill a pint pot. It built up rapidly and in the following year, 2012, the coldest and wettest summer for a hundred years, it filled a super with 30 pounds of honey during the Olympic Fortnight.

It was from Himalayan Balsam, a very pale honey with a delicious taste, prize winning. Very few colonies produced any honey in the UK during that dreadful summer.

Lesson learnt: don't reject casts, they can be very productive during the following year, since the queen will be young and vigorous. Just make sure that the swarm box isn't too large and that it doesn't smell of cider.

Joe Bleasdale
2013

INDEX

absconding swarm	87	honey flow	18
acarine	75	Horizontal Top Bar Hive	29
American Foulbrood	70	ivy honey	54
Anaphylactic shock	7	Langstroth	27
Autumn Feeding	60	larva	9
Bait Hives	45	laying workers	57
Bee Space	27	lifecycle	9
Bee suit	35	mandibles	11,18
Brood	9	mead	55
Buckfast	20	mice	76
Chrysalid	17	moving hive	31
Chrysalis	17	nadiring	27
cluster	9	National Hive	27
colony	9	Natural Beekeepers	34
comb	9	nectar	18
comb honey	51	nosema	70
combining hives	78	nucleus	27
communication	19	pheromone	19
crown board	27	piping queen	13
development times	10,11,13	pollen	18
diseases	70	population	9,23
drone	15	propagation	81
eggs	9	propolis	9
Emergency Queen Cells	14	pupa	9,10
European Foulbrood	70	queen	11
feeding	59	queen cell	13,14
fermenting honey	54	queen excluder	36,49
fondant	43	queen substance	11
frame	27	quilt	28
glands	9,11,17,19,20	robbing	48
granulated honey	54	royal jelly	11
hearing	20	semen	10
heather honey	54	senses	19
hive tool	35	sight	19
honey barrier	49	skep	27
honey extracting	50	smell	19

smoker	35
sperm	10
Sun Hive	27
supering	31
supersedure	13
swarm	11
swarm prevention	45
taste	19
temperature	9
touch	20
varroa	72
Varroa Resistant Bees	72
ventilation	72
Von Frisch	20
Warré Hive	27
wasps	76
wax cappings	50
wax moth	76
William Broughton Carr (WBC)	27
winter starvation	79
woodpeckers	76
worker	16